THE Art of Mingling

EASY, FUN, AND PROVEN TECHNIQUES FOR MASTERING ANY ROOM

JEANNE MARTINET

MJF BOOKS
NEW YORK

Published by MJF Books
Fine Communications
Two Lincoln Square
60 West 66th Street
New York, NY 10023

The Art of Mingling
Copyright © 1992 by Jeanne Martinet
ISBN 1-56731-422-8
LC Control No. 00-134271

This edition published by arrangement with St. Martin's Press, New York
Design by Diane Stevenson/Snap.Haus Graphics

Manufactured in the United States of America on acid-free paper

MJF Books and the MJF colophon are trademarks of Fine Creative Media, Inc.

10   9   8   7   6   5   4   3   2   1

To my friend Jason,
the nicest minglephobic I know

CONTENTS

Acknowledgments

I really should thank everyone with whom I have ever mingled; but in particular, I would like to extend my warm gratitude to the following people who gave me support and/or mingling tips and stories:

Meg Blackstone, Linda Brown, Millie Brawley, Eliza Button, David and Tabitha Chung, Cathy Curlett, Nicolas Dalton, Trent Duffy, Joyce Engelson, Elizabeth Geiser, Chief Gordon, Virginia Graham, Camille Hykes, Steve Kurtz, Sarah and Graham Lorimer, Tom Lunde, Scott Martinet, Margaret and Bruce McElvein, Peter and Christine Mathis, Amy Mintzer, Kent Oswald, Caroline Press, MK and Herman Raucher, Margo Ross, Claire Schapiro, Larry Schlang, and Bill Sweeney.

I would like also to offer special thanks to my kind and generous parents, Leigh and Doris Martinet; and to my agent, Teresa Cavanaugh, and my editor, Barbara Anderson.

INTRODUCTION

Y ou are at a cocktail party. The decor is fabulous, the food mouth-watering, the guests glamorous—wonderful, right?

Wrong. It's a nightmare. You want desperately to disappear. Everywhere around you are people who seem to know each other. They are talking and laughing, having a great time, while you are standing against the wall, wishing with all your heart and soul that you were somewhere else—anywhere else—but here (Beam me up, Scotty!). Two firm convictions keep you from dying on the spot: 1) There's no question about it. You are going to take the life of the (ex) friend who convinced you that you needed to expand your horizons by coming to this party, and 2) If this night ever ends, you will never, *ever* leave the safety of your home again.

An exaggeration? Maybe. But I know plenty of people, of all ages and from all walks of life, who are perfectly comfortable with the one-on-one or the small-group social interaction but confess a secret terror of medium-to-large parties of any kind. They'll do *anything* to avoid mingling. The very *idea* of having to talk to a lot of people they don't know makes them go weak in the knees. This is a shame bordering on a tragedy, because larger affairs—whether they be business or "social" functions—are potentially more exciting and energizing than small get-togethers. But because of their fear, many people waste good opportunities either by not going to a party, or by going with a colleague or companion, with whom they spend the entire time talking. Anything, they think, is better than to risk being a "wallflower," left standing all alone, looking pathetic and ridiculous. And even that is preferable to suffering the incomparable agony of being face-to-face with a stranger and not knowing what to say.

People who feel this way (and there are more of them out there than you can imagine) have a disease known as *minglephobia*. Is there a cure? Yes. Because contrary to what you might think, "making conversation," "being a social butterfly," or "working the room" is a *learned* art—a simple one—which ANYONE can master.

It's true that social skills *seem* to come more easily to some people, and there are a lucky few who are actually born mingling geniuses (in fact, I once saw a three-year-old boy work a room so well it was scary). But even the pathetically shy, the tongue-tied, and the foot-in-mouth types can learn simple techniques, tricks, lines, and maneuvers that can mean the difference between fun and misery, between a night of total humiliation and one of social ecstasy.

I've heard some people say mingling is nothing but a waste of time involving an endless stream of trivial, meaningless conversations with people you will never see again. Okay, I admit I've had my share of inane discussions about hair design or fingernail polish, which left me wondering if it was all worth it. But I've also had at least four or five ten-minute conversations that have deeply affected my life. Simply being in a room full of people who are communicating with each other is exhilarating! Just look up "mingling" in the dictionary: "to be or become mixed or united or to become closely associated; join or take part with others." Sounds stimulating, even sexy, doesn't it? It is. I know from experience.

I'll tell you a secret. Although I have always adored parties—anywhere, anytime—mingling didn't come naturally to me at all. But when I was about thirteen, I made up my mind that I would become a mingling virtuoso. I proceeded to teach myself the art over the course of years, by trial and error. I have collected tips and adapted techniques from countless friends and acquaintances. All the methods I use have been tested and honed for best results, and now I have a system that never fails. It's easy, and you can learn it, too.

There's one important thing to remember as you begin to study this time-honored art. *Your purpose in any mingling situation is to have fun.* This is an absolutely vital, hard-and-fast rule; your success as a mingler depends on this basic premise. Whether you are at a business affair or a friend's party, whether you are mingling for love or for career advancement (incidentally, I think we've all had enough of the word "networking"; I refuse to use it except in the context of fishing), your *primary* goal must be your own enjoyment. People may use mingling situations to climb the proverbial corporate ladder; but, ostensibly, their motivation for attending the event is to enjoy the company of their fellow human beings. The methods for socializing in business situations are the same as the ones for socializing in your personal life. And each of the following step-by-step techniques and lines is applicable to just about any type of gathering.

So, take a deep breath, and LET'S MINGLE!

· 1 ·

THE FIRST STEP: OVERCOMING MINGLEPHOBIA

HOW TO FAKE IT TILL YOU MAKE IT

Okay. So there you are, standing alone, frozen against the wall in a room full of people. You've just arrived, and you've already done the two things that made you look busy: taken off your coat, and said hello to your host or hostess, who has long since dashed off to greet another guest or check on the ice supply. What now?

Number one: *Don't panic*. You're not alone. Many people descend into existential angst when faced with tough mingling situations. Some people deal with their fears by withdrawing, others act nervous or clumsy. Some giggle sheepishly, some even cry. In fact, minglephobia can cause people to drink too much, eat too much, smoke too much, or—and this can really be dangerous—even *dance too much*. So it's important not to give in to your fears, especially in those first few crucial moments. Just try to relax and say to yourself, *I'm going to fake it till I make it.*

Believe it or not, this simple affirmation is an effective—almost magical—way to transform party terror into a positive outlook. Remember when you were little and you used to tell ghost stories to scare yourself and by the end of the night, you really did believe in ghosts? It was amazingly easy to fool yourself when you were a child, and it's just as easy to fool yourself as an adult. Just *pretend* to be happy to be wherever you are; make believe you are confident; simulate self-assurance—even for just ten minutes—and an amazing thing will start to happen: *you'll actually begin to feel that way,* partially because of the response you get from other people.

Let's face it. Very few people want to talk to someone who is showing outward signs of fear or depression. (That is, unless that someone is putting on an especially dramatic act or pose—usually an expert mingler in disguise—or unless he or she is of the part-the-Red-Sea physical looks minority. And this book isn't for them.) So while you will probably have at least *some* apprehension when approaching people you know little or not at all, you must practice putting it aside. Just as if you're walking out on a stage. Deep breath. Curtain up. Before you know it, you'll discover you're no longer faking it, that your fears have disappeared and you are having a good time!

Fake It Till You Make It is an attitude aid rather than a specific technique, but it's important to remember it as you begin to mingle as it is the basis of all opening gambits and entry lines. Like having the right paper—or the right software—before you begin writing, your mindset as you enter the fray is extremely important. For the first few minutes of a difficult mingling experience, what you *project* is more important than what you may be feeling.

FOUR SURVIVAL FANTASIES FOR THE TRULY TERRIFIED

Sometimes the Fake It Till You Make It mantra isn't enough when you are faced with a room full of Serious Terror Inducers. The scariest groups for me are Wall Street bankers, people at art gallery openings, high-level mafioso, fashion designers, and cast members from a flop Broadway show. But whether your own worst mingling nightmare is a gathering of yuppies, jet-setters, or celebrities, and whether you are attending a high-pressure business affair or a super chic soirée, the following survival techniques can be life savers. Certain highly awkward situations, such as your twenty-fifth high school reunion, are a different story, and do not usually call for the particular armor of the survival fantasy. These mingling fantasies are for the times when you can hardly breathe; when you can't remember your name or the name of the person who invited you; when you suddenly have no idea why you were invited, and suspect that someone's secretary must have made a horrible mistake in putting you on the guest list.

The need for these fantasies varies greatly, of course, with each individual. Extraordinarily shy people or people who haven't been out of the house for two months may use them regularly. Some people (like me) find them to be so much fun that they use them all the time for the pure kick they get out of them. But in any case, they can provide you with an instant shot of social confidence, enough to allow you to approach a group of intimidating strangers. All you need to make them work is a little imagination.

• The Naked Room •

Suppose you have just arrived at a large party. As you enter the room, you realize that 1) you don't know a soul there; 2) everyone is much more glamorous than you; and 3) the second you walked in, you lost every ounce of self-assurance you ever had.

Try this: Just pretend that everyone in the room is completely naked—*except for you.* There are variations, naturally, according to what you think makes people look the most ridiculous and powerless; some people prefer to imagine everyone in their underclothes (preferably raggedy ones); some people visualize them in only socks, shoes, ties, and jewelry. But whatever version works for you, the Naked Room fantasy can be an easy way to turn the tables when you're feeling vulnerable or exposed and is an excellent place to start to build your party confidence. Old acquaintances will wonder what the devil has put that secret smile on your face, and strangers will be intrigued by your cocky demeanor.

(Please note: This technique is for use *only* as a remedy for minglephobia. Do not misuse it!)

• The Invisible Man •

This fantasy is based on a very simple truth; something my mother used to tell me all the time. *Nobody is looking at you. Everyone is too busy worrying about himself.* While this may not be 100 percent true, it is mostly true. The Invisible Man fantasy merely capitalizes on this basic fact, taking it one step further.

Ready? You're just *not there.* You don't exist. Do you think someone's looking at you, wondering snidely why no one is talking to you? You're wrong; they're looking right through you. They're looking at the food table, at the wall, at another guest. Remember in the 1933 film *The Invisible Man,* when Claude Rains took off his bandages and was totally transparent? What power he had! How he laughed! (Some mingling students may want to use as their model Lamont Cranston, the famous "Shadow" of radio days. "The *Shadow* knows . . .") Now, invisible as you are, you are free to unselfconsciously walk around the room, looking at everyone, looking at the wallpaper, the paintings—the whole scene—with

4

total relaxation. This gives you time to catch your breath, psychologically, until you feel ready to become visible again and enter the conversational clique of your choice. (*Warning*: Those tending toward isolationism may want to be careful with this one; you don't want to stay invisible for too long. I suggest timing yourself for the first couple of tries. *Reappearance is an absolute must*.)

• The Buddy System •

Remember in elementary school when you went on field trips, and your teacher used to make you line up with a partner so that no one would get lost? In my school, they called this the "Buddy System." Well, here you are now, feeling virtually "lost" in this room full of intimidating strangers. How can you possibly get up the nerve to speak to anyone?

Easy. You and your best buddy *will go together*. Tell yourself that just behind you, over your right shoulder, your very best friend in the whole world is moving with you through the room, listening to everything you say. Voilà: instant calm. After all, your friend loves you, right? Understands you? And probably will have a lot of the same opinions of the people you meet as you do. When you talk, you will be able to imagine this friend smiling at everything you say, offering encouragement and approval. And if by chance you are snubbed by some uneducated dolt, you'll hear your friend whisper in your ear, "What a jerk!"

Once again, however, there is an admonition attached to this trick. Don't get carried away and actually *speak* to your imaginary friend (at least not so anyone can notice).

• The Lucky Star •

This is kind of the Invisible Man fantasy in reverse. It may seem drastic to some people, but I find it so effective, as well as so much fun, that I highly recommend it, especially for the more adventuresome mingling novice. Don't forget, these fantasy techniques are specifically designed for *initial* courage; to get you to take that first step, to transform you from a wall-flower with an inferiority complex into a participating, mingling member of the party. So try this:

Be someone else, just for a little while. This might seem a bit radical, especially since other people have probably been telling you for decades to "be yourself," but if you're standing there at the party, terrified, halfway wishing you were somebody else anyway, then why not do it? The person that you are is giving you a lot of trouble right now, and is obviously not the least bit happy about where it is. So pick a favorite celebrity, someone whose poise, posture, or personality you particularly admire, and just . . . slip into him or her. When done right, this technique works much more quickly than the other survival fantasies, because of the mingling power most people attribute to stars—power that instantly becomes accessible to you.

When I was a smoker (more about cigarettes as props later), I would often use Bette Davis for the Lucky Star fantasy, especially for really tough rooms. I would visualize her in one of her movie roles, usually *All About Eve,* and pretty soon I would sense my eyebrows going up slightly and my body relaxing, as I surveyed the social battlefield with a truly languid amusement. As Bette Davis, I would not just be *ready* to mingle, I'd be positively *hungry* for it.

No one, by the way, ever looked over at me and screamed, "Look at that weird woman pretending to be Bette Davis!" because no one, of course, ever noticed the difference. They merely saw a confident—perhaps even interesting—woman. Likewise, no one will be able to tell what *you* are doing when you use this technique. After all, that's why these are called "fantasies"—they're *secret.* And you don't *have* to use a celebrity. You can, if you want, pretend to be someone you know in real life, someone who is never ill at ease (or, more likely, who never *seems* to be ill at ease—they probably feel the same as you do inside, of course). The only guideline is that you must choose someone you know pretty well; the better you know this person, the easier it is to assume his or her persona.

Some favorite Lucky Stars for women: Bette Davis, Mae West (especially if you're the kind of person who really feels powerful with your hand on your hip!), Ingrid Bergman, Liza Minnelli, Vivien Leigh (as Scarlett, of course), Bette Midler, Katharine Hepburn, Madonna, Connie Chung, Jane Pauley, Gloria Steinem, Jackie Onassis, and Grace Kelly. Men can use: William Powell, Fred Astaire, Cary Grant, Humphrey Bogart, David Niven, Jack Nicholson, Harrison Ford, Arsenio Hall, Ted Turner, Peter Jennings, or even JFK. Please note: It's best not to use people who are charismatic *but* may actually be frightening (such as Richard Nixon, Peter Lorre, Vincent Price, or Cruella De Ville).

Each of these survival fantasies will take some practice, particularly if you've never tried anything like this before. But believe me, they *will* help, especially if you are a person who tends to freeze, to one degree or another, at the very beginning of a difficult mingling experience. You may find, also, that you develop your own personalized survival fantasy—one that works better for you than any of the ones I have outlined—and that's fine, of course. But do stay away from extremely malevolent fantasies; they simply don't work as far as mingling goes.

And now, bolstered by the survival fantasy of your choice, you are ready to enter the field, to approach a person or persons—to get to the actual "meat" of mingling.

Choosing Your First Clique

As in any game or art, deciding where to begin is very important. Every party, every large gathering, has its bright lights, its superstar mingle circles, its personality power points. Should you forge ahead and go right for the loudest, laughingest, most powerful enclave of people in the room?

Absolutely not! Not unless you consider yourself in the intermediate to advanced level in the art of mingling. After all, you've just gone through at least one survival fantasy to get you this far, and you don't want to blow it by being shot down by the brightest member of the party. Instead, you must first get in some relatively safe practice.

• Practice Your Mingle on a Nerd •

That's right. Scope out the sorriest, wimpiest, limpest group in the whole room. This of course will vary from party to party; it's all relative. Usually it's a semi-quiet group of people, perhaps not as attractive as the other guests, and often badly or inappropriately dressed. Lots of times you can identify them by their lost, sheepish expressions or shuffling stances, or by the way they appear to be fascinated by one of the wall fixtures. At any rate, you must think of this first cluster (or first several clusters, depending on how much practice you need), as your sketch pad, your scratch paper, your dress rehearsal. Something that really *doesn't count.*

Keep in mind as you approach this group: You are about to interact with the party's lowest common denominator, and though their responses to you might be educational, your main purpose is to listen to *yourself,* learn how certain gambits work, how they feel to you. Did a certain line come naturally to you, or did it sound rehearsed? Was it perhaps executed with the wrong inflection?

You can try out mingling techniques you'd ordinarily never dare to try, knowing that you are risking very little. Of course, you must remember, when you are practicing your mingle in such a group, that the reaction you get is not necessarily the reaction you can expect from one of the brighter circles. Nevertheless, the opportunity to practice is invaluable and should be taken advantage of in every possible situation.

A friend of mine was absolutely appalled when I explained to him this particular method. At first I thought he was outraged that I would callously describe other human beings as "nerds," but I was quite wrong.

"How can you suggest such a thing?" he ranted, "I'd be afraid of being branded a nerd myself if I were to be seen *talking* to nerds!" This is an understandable concern, but keep the following in mind: First of all there aren't likely to be that many real nerds to choose from; mostly it will be a matter of *not* starting with the glitterati. Secondly, if there *are* authentic nerds in attendance, most people will not classify you just by seeing you talking to them. A good mingler by his very nature talks to as many people at the party as possible, and certainly people won't label you unless you are attached to a bunch of dweebs for a long time, which is emphatically not recommended. There's also the possibility of attending an all-nerd affair, at which you can, if you want, try out some *really* adventurous mingling maneuvers (though you may also want to ask yourself why *you* were invited).

Occasionally, you may find yourself in the unfortunate position of being at a "nerdless" social gathering, where *everyone there is a bright light*. When this happens, you'll have to do without the luxury of stress-free practice and just dive right in.

• Judging a Book by Its Cover •

If there are no nerds on whom to practice, or if you simply don't feel like talking to them, there is another very effective way to choose a safe and easy mingling target. I learned this

9

method while watching my father, a musician, at a rather stuffy party of mostly lawyers and bankers. He stood there, scoping out the party, not talking to anyone, for about fifteen minutes.

"Typical musician," I thought to myself, "totally antisocial." Suddenly, he made a beeline for a man standing in the corner. Before long, the two of them were engrossed in conversation, laughing away. Curious, I joined them ("Hi, Dad" is, by the way, always a good entrance line!). The "subject" my father had picked was a journalist, and turned out to be rather a kindred spirit to my father. I noted that they talked on and off for the entire evening.

Later I asked my father how he had chosen this man to talk to, out of all the people at the party. "Easy," he replied. "He was the only man there without a suit and tie." My father, who never wears a suit and tie if he can help it, had selected his first mingling subject on the basis of similar taste in clothes, on the assumption that the man's attire was an indication of a creative personality. And he was right!

Fact one: You can often tell a lot about a person by appearance. Fact two: It is almost always easier to converse with someone who is similar to you rather than to someone who is dissimilar. Therefore, if you choose a person who is dressed as you are, or even as you would *like* to be dressed, your chances of a comfortable—maybe even fun—exchange are increased. And because you are at the very beginning of your mingling and you're nervous, it's vital that your first couple of encounters go well, or you may give up and go home before you've even begun to mingle.

• The Safety of Numbers •

When making that all-important decision of whom to approach first, keep in mind one of the simplest, oldest maxims in the history of social interaction: *There is safety in numbers.*

Whether you are making a gentle kind of approach or a boisterously dramatic entrance, your chances of avoiding total disgrace are statistically better with a larger group of people.

Either everyone will notice you as soon as you enter the circle, and because there are so many people, when you throw a line out, some of them (at least one, anyhow) are bound to be polite; or *no one* will notice you joining the group, giving you ample time to listen, digest the different personalities, and choose an appropriate opening line—or escape from the clique totally unscathed, a virtual mingling virgin.

In general, the larger the group, the larger your range of options. Perhaps most important, in a large group you will almost difinitely *not* die the horrible death of awkward silence, something that *can* happen to you when you are involved with a cluster of two or even three people.

Of course, the best defense against awkward silences is a great opening.

·2·

OPEN SESAME: MAKING A SUCCESSFUL ENTRANCE

RESTRAINING ORDERS

ow you've selected a mingling target group and you're ready to make your entrance. Before we get to the specific openings, there are a couple of things to consider.

• To Shake or Not to Shake •

No, this is not about how to stop trembling. It's about that age-old custom of hand-clasping, traditionally thought to be a matter of etiquette.

I have found it in most mingling situations—even at business parties—usually a very risky business. Often it interrupts any conversation that is already flowing in the circle of people you are entering, not to mention that many people are holding drinks, food, cigarettes, or other items in their hands. It also can punctuate, more loudly than you may want, the fact that you have officially joined the group

And so, although most of us are trained by our parents that it is polite to shake hands with a person when meeting them, my rule for entering a group of more than one or two people is *not to shake* unless introduced to someone by a third person. There are exceptions to this rule: Some approaches or opening lines necessitate a handshake, and, of course, sometimes someone else initiates a handshake.

Men: This is going to be hard for you. For some reason, men *love* to shake hands, anytime, anywhere. Sew your hands to your pockets if you have to, but *don't stick out that hand* unless someone else sticks his or hers out first.

• A Word About Smiling •

Everyone has his own personal "smile style," but there are some general rules to follow about smiling at the particular time you are entering a conversational clique. Unless your approach involves interruption, I recommend that you either do not smile, or that you use a closed-mouth smile. A toothy smile can seem too cheery, and there is something decidedly off-putting, even odd, about a total stranger approaching you with an enormous grin on his or her face. It's distracting, to say the least, and makes the recipient wonder if he's being laughed at. On the other hand, a closed or toothless smile is mysterious, sophisticated, and subtle. Remember, you don't want to scare off the group you're joining!

As usual, there are exceptions to this rule, but you'd probably know if you are one of them. For example, I know someone whose smile is so powerful, whose teeth are so white, that it almost hurts your eyes. His smile radiates personality anywhere he goes, and people actually gather around him just to warm themselves by his pearly whites. He floats in and out of groups without following the closed-smile rule, without knowing the first thing about mingling, in fact. Obviously, if you have a smile like this, you should use it, teeth and all, as much as you want to (maybe *more* than you want to!).

In any case, you shouldn't *worry* too much about your smile, as too much worrying about it can cause unnatural things to happen to your mouth. Most people, anyway, don't realize when they are smiling and how, and that's perfectly okay. But if you have trouble remembering the rule about smiling, here's a little rhyme to memorize:

> *When going in,*
> *No toothful grin.*
> *Use, for a while*
> *the closed-mouth smile.*
> *After clever remarks,*
> *the lips may part.*

THE FOUR BASIC ENTRANCE MANEUVERS
• The Honest Approach •

After you've tried this and experienced the response, you'll be astonished at how few people use it. I first tried this opening on a wild impulse when I was feeling overwhelmingly lost at a very stuffy publication party for a novelist. I didn't know a soul, and most of the guests were clustered in tight, closed groups of two or three—the hardest kind to enter smoothly. I slipped into a survival fantasy for a few moments, then marched right up to a pleasant-looking man who was totally engrossed in conversation. I stood beside him long enough for him to look over at me (maybe one or two minutes, which can be a lifetime in this situation) and said, "Excuse me, I hope you don't mind my coming up to you like this, but I don't know a single person here. My name is. . . ."

At the time, I thought it was a rather dangerous ploy. Imagine my delight when this fellow, whose name turned out to be Peter, smiled as if I had just handed him a million dollars and told me that he had always wanted to use that approach at a party but had always been too nervous, that he thought it was great that I just introduced myself that way. We ended up having a long and enjoyable conversation. About a week after the party, I actually received a letter from Peter, thanking me for reminding him about an "important interpersonal skill"! This is, I'll admit, an extreme case. But I have used the technique many times since then, and it has always worked, to varying degrees (though I never got any more fan mail about it!).

The honest approach works because it strikes a familiar chord in almost everyone, and because it immediately offers power to the person you are approaching, creating a non-threatening situation. The only trick is, you have to sound sincere. To *sound* sincere, you have to *be* at least partially sincere. So it is best if you use this approach only when you truly don't know anyone at the event. The other thing to remember about the honest approach is that you should use it only once or twice at a specific party. If you use the line on anyone who has already seen you talking intimately to someone at the party, you obviously lose credibility.

Note: This approach *is* one where it's okay, even helpful, to use a handshake. This is because it is *interruptive* in nature, and any blatant interruption is already so disruptive that a handshake can act as a communicative salve.

As with many mingling techniques, the honest approach will work best if tailored to suit your personality. But whatever words you use, you're bound to have fun finding out that sometimes honesty *is* the best policy.

• The Fade-in •

This thief-in-the-night gambit is usually too passive and too slow for my taste, but I know many people who swear by it.

Move as unobtrusively as you can up to the circle of your choice. Listen carefully to everything that's being said as you draw near. The idea is not to be noticed entering the enclave, but to become an intrinsic part of it before they realize you're a newcomer. If you pay close attention to the conversation while you are fading in, you'll be able to contribute to it at an appropriate place, as if you had been there all along, taking part in the discussion. And if by chance you are discovered before your Fade-in is complete, you will, with any luck, have heard enough to make a pertinent comment and gain immediate acceptance.

The key to the Fade-in is acting as if you *absolutely* belong there, as if you have been an integral part of this group for hours, as if talking to this specific set of people is what you do for a living. You'll find it is incredibly easy to convince people just by acting as if something is true.

Warning: Be sure to complete your Fade-in. It's of vital importance that within a fairly short period of time, you either complete entry—that is, say something—or move on to another group. The tendency will be, if you're insecure about meeting new people, just to hang around the periphery, listening and not joining in. This is not mingling! Don't be a party ghost!

• The Flattery Entrée •

This method may seem self-explanatory, but there's a right way to flatter and a wrong way, especially in mingling situations. While everyone responds to certain kinds of flattery,

16

there are other kinds that can bomb in a nuclear way. Here's a short quiz to find out how much you already know about flattery:

OPENING LINE   SHOULD YOU USE IT?

1. *"Excuse me, but I couldn't help noticing*   Yes No
   your beautiful dress (or suit). I love it!
   Where did you get it?"
2. *"Hello! Those are the most fabulous*   Yes No
   earrings!"
3. *"Excuse me, but you have a body of a*   Yes No
   god(goddess). Do you work out?"
4. *"Pardon me, you all seem like such a nice*   Yes No
   group of people. Do you mind if I join
   you?"
5. *"Hi. (whispering) Do you mind if I talk to*   Yes No
   you guys? I don't want to sound mean, but
   you're the only people here who seem
   interesting."
6. *"Well! Do you mind if I join this*   Yes No
   illustrious circle of high-powered shakers
   and movers?"
7. *"Hello! I heard the laughter from across the*   Yes No
   room. Since you all must be the funniest
   people here, I decided I'd come over and be
   amused."

Now let's see how you did.

1. **The correct answer to this one is no.** The main thing about flattery is that it's often better not to use it than to risk going overboard. Unless someone is wearing a getup that is definitely a costume, meant to draw comments (and you'd better be sure about this), it's too personal—even threatening—to *open* with this kind of remark. To say you

17

love someone's suit is basically the same as saying you like the way he looks, his body, his style, and that's simply too forward for the Flattery Entrée. After you've talked to the person for a while, then perhaps you can try this line. But not for an opening.

2. **Yes.** It's much more appropriate to comment on someone's accessories. It's a tribute to her taste without being too personal. This is also a smart opening because you can follow it up by asking where the person got the earrings, and, depending on her answer ("A trip to China," "My boyfriend's mother," "I made them from stuff I found on the street"), you can get a good five or ten minutes' conversation out of it, especially if you're ready to let the response lead you off into exciting new territory! **Warning:** Make sure the person is actually *wearing* earrings before you use this line.

3. **Definitely not.** Not only will this be taken as a come-on, but also it's way too strong, too personal, and too gushy. Gushing is never a good idea unless you already know the person, and even then it's iffy.

4. **This one may seem at first glance to be a possibility, but the answer is no.** First of all, though it seems to smack of the honest approach, you can't possibly know these people are nice since you haven't talked to them yet; the comment will seem insincere. Secondly, it's too *wimpy,* too "gee-whiz." A wit in the group may shoot you down with "Well you're wrong, Baby. We're all a *terrible* lot—you don't want to associate with us."

5. **No.** Believe it or not, I thought this might work in some crowds, so last New Year's Eve I tried it out. Boy, was I sorry. What a disaster! The two guys looked at me like I was a leper, and while I was trying to figure out if there was something wrong with my delivery or what, I heard a scandalized voice right behind me, where I thought no one was standing, say, "Of all the nerve!" Horror of hor-

rors, someone had overheard me. It took some pretty fancy footwork to recover. In any case, even if you aren't overheard, it's a bad idea for two reasons: the people you are addressing may be good friends of other people at the party, and may therefore be insulted; and it's simply too negative a comment for most people to accept as a compliment.

6. **Yes *and* no.** If the group you are trying to enter is made up of business peers who are no more powerful in your field than you, this is a fine, lighthearted piece of flattery. However, if the circle *does* contain "shakers and movers" of a much higher professional level than you, then this is a terrible idea. Such a group must be entered carefully, in order not to draw too much attention to the fact that one of the lower echelon has had the nerve to join it.

7. **Yes.** This is the kind of Flattery Entrée that can work (assuming you are approaching a circle of people who have really been laughing). It makes the people feel good without being threatening or too personal in any way, and it's believable, since you really can be drawn to people by their good energy. As with all openings, you will want to adapt it to your personality, using language that is comfortable for you.

Keep in mind that using flattery in an opening line and using it after you are involved in conversation are very different things. While it's often true that "flattery will get you everywhere," until you get to know what kind of people you are dealing with, you have to be very careful with the butter.

• The Sophistication Test •

There's no better way to find out what kind of person you're talking to than this, and it's also an excellent icebreaker. I use the Sophistication Test often, especially when I'm feeling particularly out of my element. It's a quick, sure-fire method of figuring out what kind of subject matter, what tone, and what level of familiarity is appropriate. Please note that this opener must be directed to only one or two people at a time; if you are entering a larger group, use the Test on one person in the group. The question that I've found works best is:

"How did you get here?"

This question can obviously be taken many different ways, which is the whole purpose of the test. If the person answers, "In a cab," you can relax a bit (although you might prepare to be a little bored); this person isn't going to throw you any curves and will probably stay more or less on the surface of things. If he or she replies, "Well, I knew the hostess's ex-husband, so I guess that's how I rated," you know you've got a fun person with whom you can kid around somewhat. Even "Would you like to see my birth certificate?" is good news; it's a sign of a witty conversationalist. But watch out for the guy or gal who says, "My father caught my mother on a good night"—this one's big trouble and you've got to really hold on to your hat.

There are only two other types of responses, and both of them indicate immediate escape. One of them is "What business is it of yours?" and the other is "I don't know." The former signifies out-of-control hostility—a great detriment to mingling—and the latter is evidence of mental impairment of some kind (or heavy-duty drugs).

You may want to concoct your own Sophistication Test question or use one of the ones listed below, but be sure whoever you use it on hasn't heard you giving the same test to another guest. You don't want anyone to realize you are conducting pre-conversational research!

"So what d'ya' think?"

"How do you fit into the picture?"

"Well, what's your role in all this?"

20

"Hey—what's it all about anyway?"

"What experience have you had?"

"What's your story?"

Opening Lines That Really Work

If you choose not to use the Honest Approach, the Fade-in, the Flattery Entrée, or the Sophistication Test, you may want to employ one of the following opening lines. Along with my own tried-and-true favorites, which I have listed below, you may want to record your own pet lines in the blank spaces provided. Most people think of great opening lines—hours after the party has ended! Write them down here for easy reference so that next time, one will roll off your tongue like magic. Just remember to follow a few simple rules:

1. Never, never, never (*trust me*) use "What do you do for a living?" as an opening line. It's not only boring, it's dangerous. The person may have just been fired, or he may be a gangster or an insurance salesman; but whatever he is, unless it's something you find fascinating or know something about, it can be a real dead end. It also may seem to some people as if you are trying to find out if they are worth your time. In fact, once the person's told you what he does for a living, you are bound by the rules of courtesy to stick around and chat with him about it; you can't very well say "Oh, how interesting," and then make a hasty exit!

2. Those who mingle best, mingle alone. While you may have your *imaginary* "buddy" with you (if you're using the Buddy System) you don't want to actually mingle with a mate or a friend, unless, of course, one of you knows most

of the people there and is introducing the other one around. Occasionally you meet someone at the beginning of the party who is a little minglephobic, too, and it's tempting to go around the room together; after all, it seems less scary that way. This is definitely a no-no. It's too hard to assimilate into clusters when you are a pair; it can be threatening and, at the same time, it just looks wimpy.

3. Whatever words are coming out of your mouth, say them with strength and confidence. If you find you're not getting anywhere with a certain line, but you can't understand why, try it on someone else with a different inflection or a different accompanying facial expression. Above all, don't give up! Don't forget, 90 percent of America has minglephobia, so you are not alone.

Practice these opening lines in the mirror, (if that kind of thing appeals to you,) or on a friend or loved one at home. Then the words will just flow naturally out of your mouth when you need them for mingling.

"How's life treating you?"

"Am I interrupting something confidential?"

"So what was your day like today?"

"Hi. What's your connection to this thing?"

"Is there anyone here who is about to go on vacation or who just got back from one? I'd love to relax vicariously."

"A little birdie told me this was the place to get the most up-to-date [name of your business] news."

"What's the password?"

"Hello, someone told me that I should come and talk to you."

"If you're who I think you are, I've just heard the most wonderful things about you!"

"If you're who I think you are, I've just heard the most terrible things about you."

"You're not going to believe this, but the hostess [host] seems to think we're related!"

"I just can't believe how big [beautiful/dark/noisy] it is here, can you?"

"This music reminds me of my childhood [high school/college days]"

"Every time I come to one of these things I wonder about the human race."

"Hello! Hey, doesn't [name of host or hostess] look great tonight?"

"Excuse me, but what is that wonderful-looking stuff you're eating [drinking]?"

"Isn't this [type of food you are eating or have tried] delicious?"

"Excuse me, but my friend and I were having an argument about mingling and she bet me I couldn't walk up to you all and immediately join in . . . no, don't look at her! . . . please just smile—that's good—and talk to me so I can win."

"Hello! I don't know any of you, I know, but I'm practicing my mingling tonight."

"_____"

"_____"

"_____"

"_____"

Naturally, the success of these lines depends a lot on your delivery. Some of them require an ironic tone, some call for enthusiasm, some an air of puzzlement. Some of them are better suited to some people than others. Select the ones that seem most like something you would say, and remember that you can always alter them slightly to fit your own style. But don't be afraid to try something daring once in a while. It's not going to kill you, and it may *slay* them!

·3·

NOW WHAT?: TOOLS AND RULES FOR CONTINUING THE CONVERSATION

N ow that you've chosen your first target group and bravely uttered your opening line, you may be wondering, "Now what? What happens *after* the opening?" Well, it's up to you. You've got four options:

1. You can hang about silently, listening to the other people in the group talk, satisfied that you've actually pulled off an opening (in other words, stop mingling).

2. You can exit immediately upon completing the opening gambit, using one of the techniques that will be described in chapter 4.

3. You can give up entirely and go home.

4. You can segue smoothly into a conversation with one or more of the people with whom you are now standing.

Obviously, the most rewarding choice, from a mingling standpoint, is option four, which is, for many people, the hardest part of the mingling experience. Getting in to a group is one thing; maintaining your own in that group is another. Even a smashingly successful opening line is only the beginning, like getting accepted into college. Now you actually have to *go* to college. In fact, many people are just as terror-stricken after a *successful* opening line as after one that flubs, even though they presumably now have the other person(s)' attention and everything is A-okay. A good response to your opening may give you a temporary high, but then minglephobia usually sets in again. "Oh my God," you think frantically to yourself, "What do I talk about with this person?" Don't worry. This chapter should give you enough ammunition so you won't ever again end up tongue-tied, red-faced, or sweaty-palmed. It's much easier to find things to say than we have been conditioned to think. There's a whole world of subject matter out there, and there are some easy methods to keep a variety of topics at your fingertips.

But first of all, let's take care of the worst-case scenario.

Recovering from a Muffed Opening

Sometimes your opening line will fall flat on the ground and just lie there, dead. This can be demoralizing, but here are some things you can do:

- **Pretend it never happened.** Just start over with another opening line. For example, suppose you chose the Fade-in entrance, but you're noticed before you get a chance to listen to the conversation and complete the maneuver. Everyone has stopped talking and is looking at you. *Don't panic.* You can switch immediately to the honest approach, the Flattery Entrée, the Sophistication Test (this one's harder with a large group), or deliver one of the opening lines you've memorized. It's really not difficult to move quickly to another opening gambit, and it's important to know that it is *not unusual* to use more than one opening. The essential thing is not to lose your confidence. Don't let it be known that you are disappointed your opening missed its mark. The survival fantasies can really help at a time like this.

- **Be honest.** Let's say you used the line (see page 22) "Am I interrupting something confidential?" and you get the number-one killer reaction: They exchange looks with each other that say "What a bimbo!" and offer no verbal response of any kind. In other words, the Silent Treatment. Once in a while someone may respond to this particular line with a "Yes!" in which case you should apologize politely and move on. But in the case of the Silent Meanies, I suggest you laugh (if you can, or at least smile) and say "Well! I can see that's the last time I try that line!" or "I'm sorry, did I offend somebody?" It indicates that you can't be intimidated and that you know *you* haven't done anything wrong.

- **Lie.** In the same situation as above, for example, say, "Look, I know that sounded rather odd, but I just had the most embarrassing experience; some people over there told me they were having a private conversation, *thank-you-very-much,* and they didn't want to be disturbed. So I thought I'd better check this time!" Or, if you've approached someone from behind, you can always use the old standard, "Oh, excuse me! I thought you were somebody else." Or—and this is my favorite lie for this situation—"Well, don't look at me that way! I was warned before I came over here that you guys were unapproachable. Everyone *else* is too afraid to break in!" This is a good ploy for two reasons: 1) It's a strong bluff, and is, in fact, a continuation of the opening line itself. From a power standpoint, which is something the Silent Meanies are almost *always* into, it's positive and will be respected. Even the most aloof will have to deny it with at least one sentence ("I beg your pardon, but we were not trying to be standoffish; we were just talking"), which is

26

enough to let you change the subject or withdraw gracefully. 2) Most anyone with an ego will want to know who at the party has been gossiping about them, and you can have a lot of fun not telling them—because of course you won't be able to—and they'll think you're protecting the gossiper and the conversation can really get rolling along—with you in control.

- **Be funny.** You really have to be careful with humor, which is something I'll address later in this chapter. But for some people, having their opening bomb is so devastating that the only way for them to keep up their confidence and go on is to strike back with a funny line, like a comedian does with hecklers. Sadly, if you *are* dealing with real snobs like the Silent Meanies, sometimes this is the only way to handle them. Take the same example of the "confidential" line and the worst-case, icy reaction. You might be able to win them with "Are you going to talk to me or am I under arrest?" Or how about "Sorry, I didn't see your 'do not disturb' sign up." Or even "Has the stock market crashed?" or "What? Is my face blue or something?" You might try "Ah, *Pardonez-moi. Vous ne parlez pas Anglais?. . . Parlez Français?. . . . Español?. . .Deutsch? . . .*" Or, if you're really ready to burn your bridges: "Oh, I'm sorry, I thought you were humans."

- **Leave.** If the response is really as hostile as the extreme case I've suggested, your best move may be just to leave these bozos in the dust, unless there's some pressing reason to try further (for example, if one of them happens to be a major business contact, or someone you're hoping to interview). Try someone else, and use a different line, at least for a while. Some lines are just wrong for some parties, and some lines may be ill suited to you. Don't be discouraged.

CAREER TALK: YES OR NO?

Assuming your opening succeeds or that you recover your balance sufficiently after a muffed opening, you're still going to need some ready topics for when the conversation lags (or stops completely. I don't want to frighten you but this may happen a lot if you're an inexperienced mingler). Ideally, you want each interaction to last at least ten minutes—that's optimum mingle time—and usually the dialogue surrounding the opening will last no longer than three minutes. So what do you do when the fervor of the opening dies down, and the awkward cone of silence begins to descend?

Most people automatically leap right into "So what do you do for a living?" or more often, "What do *you* do?" as if their own occupation has already been the subject of much exciting deliberation at the party.

Please believe me when I say that this is a mingling no-no. When and where to talk "career-ese" is a debatable issue, but I do not recommend it *until and unless you have already established a rapport with the person(s).* A lot of people will disagree with me on this. After all, it goes against a golden rule of conversation that has been drilled into our heads, and that for the most part, serves us very well: People like to talk about themselves. This is, of course, basically true, and if you can't think of anything else, asking about someone's career certainly may be preferable to stuttering or fainting. In other words, it's a perfectly acceptable survival tactic. But you should be aware of the possible consequences and pitfalls.

- The person's occupation may be something really BORING, and something he or she just *loves* to talk about—for hours. This can be no fun at all, and makes you susceptible to what I call the "Glaze-out," which is similar to being hypnotized, except that it's not relaxing or particularly good for you in any way. It's almost impossible to mingle when you're in the grip of the Glaze-out. When it happens to me, I find that I can't concentrate at all on what's being said (much less say anything myself except "Uh-huh") and that I usually become transfixed by a small section of the person's face.

- The person's occupation may be something REPULSIVE to you. He could be a proctologist, or a mortician, or a hair-transplant technician, and what are you going to say then? A friend of mine who is a strict vegetarian told me about one time at a large party when she introduced herself to an interesting-looking man and then right away asked him what he did.

"I'm a butcher," he said, smiling proudly.

"Oh . . . ah . . . I . . . how interesting," my friend managed to reply, blanching.

"Yep. Best and biggest butcher in town." He went on to describe in gruesome detail what his day had entailed. "Say, what's the matter?" he asked after several minutes. "You look a little green."

"Excuse me, won't you?" my friend finally squeaked. That was the end of that conversation. Her hasty exit would have been much less embarrassing if she had talked to the man a little longer *before* she brought up professions. As it was, it seemed as if she introduced herself and then immediately bolted. Remember that when you bring up this subject, you actually do not have any idea *what* subject you are bringing up!

- The person's answer may be something DEPRESSING. Let's say you've used flattery as your entrance. You're all smiles and cheer from delivering the compliment, and then you ask "What do you do?" Suppose the person says with a quiver in his or her lip, "Well, actually, I'm between jobs at the moment, and I, well, today I thought I had gotten this job but . . . I didn't." This isn't a total disaster, of course, but it's not the greatest thing in the world to work with, as you almost have to come back with, "Oh, I'm sorry to hear that. What field are you in?" and you're going to have to hear some real downer minutes before you can change the subject. The answer could also be something that's just depressing *to you*. The person could be in charge of putting animals to sleep at the A.S.P.C.A.

- The person's occupation may be EMBARRASSING to you. Quite a few people I know, for example, would be made very uncomfortable by the following responses:

  "I'm the hostess's gynecologist."

  "I'm a sex surrogate."

29

"I'm a female impersonator."

"I work at Kentucky Fried Chicken."

"I'm a urine collector for an insurance company."

"I'm a stripper."

"Come over to my place and I'll show you."

The point is, your innocent question could leave you in the position of wanting out desperately, before you've said more than two sentences. And beware: *The sooner it is after you've started the conversation, the harder it is to escape.* Also, if you ask this question to more than one person, it often means the destruction of the group as a unit. One person answers, and because of the nature of the dialogue, some or all of the others can use your entrance into this subject to escape, which they will do, especially if they've already discovered the person is a bore. Now you're really stuck, as it is much harder to escape from one person than from many. At the very least, you've lessened your chances of having witty repartee or a back-and-forth among the whole group you've just taken great pains to enter. So before you jump into career talk, find out a little more about this person (or people) first. **Note:** the Sophistication Test sometimes works even better as a second line than it does as a first.

If you *must* talk careers right away, try a career *semi-query*. For instance, say: "How about this darned economy?" or "Did you come here directly from work?" That way, it opens up the field for career talk, but you have a little safety zone to protect yourself in case something dreadful happens.

As far as career talk goes, there are more exceptions to the rule than in any other area of mingling. For one thing, none of my warnings apply if you are at a specific business function such as a company party or your industry's annual convention. Also, there are many situations in which you can tell right away—for a wide variety of reasons—that it is a safe question and one you are even *expected* to ask. At any rate, in most cases it's certainly not the worst thing you can do, by any means. I'm merely urging you to remember the dangers and consider your options before you commit to this. There's so much more to talk about, so many other ways to really enjoy mingling!

AN ABECEDARY FOR THOSE AT LOSS FOR WORDS

Okay, so what *do* you talk about, now that you're standing there with nothing but a blank computer screen in your mind, and you can't seem to find the button to make anything appear? We've all been in this position, where twenty seconds of silence can seem like an hour. Even though you are probably not alone in your terror, as obviously no one else is saying anything either, it is undeniably *your* responsibility to get things going, since you are the one who has approached *them*.

We all know there are literally millions of subjects from which to choose: observations about the party, about current events; questions about the person's background or connection to the host or hostess; and, if it's a business affair, remarks about whatever may be new or exciting in your profession. But often the problem is how to pull something out of the air when you're stumped. So before we go any further, I'm going to offer you a very simple way—a trick, really—to think of a good topic.

When you were a child, did you ever memorize things for a history or geography class by using word-association games? My mother was crazy about this study technique, and I can remember listening to her coaching my brother with "What's the capital of Maryland? It's such a *merry land* that everyone in it gets *an apple*. Annapolis!" Sound ridiculous? Maybe, but it worked, and while this process might not suit everyone, you'll never draw a blank again if you can master this handy, miniature mingling manual for the subject-starved minglephobic.

Here's how to use it: After you have completed your opening, if you now know the name of the person or one of the people in the group, use the first letter of his or her name to remind you of one of the twenty-six key topics below. For example, if you've just met someone named Alice, think "A", which should make you think of the word "art." If you don't know anyone's name yet, use the color of someone's jacket or blouse to pick a letter (e.g., tan, "T"). Use hair or eye color, or the last word that was just said to you. It really doesn't matter what you use to choose the letter; you can just start with "A" at the beginning of the night and work your way through the alphabet, if you want. The important thing is speed. It has to look as if you are just one of those people who has a fascinating mind, able to leap from one interesting subject to another. You can deliver the line in the form it is given in the Abecedary, or you can use any of the following lead-ins:

"I was just saying to someone that . . ."

"It's interesting how . . ."

"Have you ever noticed. . .(the Andy Rooney lead-in)

"What do you think about. . ."

"What do you think about. . ." (my favorite: It implies the topic has already been a great success)

"I can't believe . . ."

Warning: When using the Abecedary, do not, under any circumstances, either say the alphabet out loud or ask someone how to spell his or her name in order to remember a subject. It's a dead giveaway you're using some kind of a mingler's aide.

Letter	Sample lines
A is for **Art**	*"Don't you think when Steve works a room it's an art form?"*
	"Look at all these people; I like looking at people more than any art in any museum I've ever seen!"

Letter	Sample lines
	"Do you suppose the art hanging on a wall genuinely affects the conversation of the people beside that wall?"
B is for **Baby**	*"I can't believe how many babies there are now at parties."*
	"What do you think a party like this would look like to a baby?"
	"When I get home I'm just going to baby myself!"
C is for **Cat**	*"Did you see a cat in here?"*
	"Are you a cat person or a dog person?"
	"Can you help me out? I'm trying to decide what to name my new cat."
D is for **Danger**	*"Don't you think it's dangerous to put all these [name of your business or profession] people in the same room?"*
	"There's danger in the air tonight."
	"What is the international sign for danger?"
E is for **Energy**	*"The energy is really good at this party, isn't it?"*
	"I don't know why, but I'm very low energy tonight."
	"How much energy do you think it took to make this party possible?"

Letter	Sample lines
F is for **Food**	*"Have you tried the food?"*
	"Don't let me have any more food."
	"Everything in our lives really revolves around food, doesn't it?"
G is for **Glowing** ...	*"Don't you think [name of host or hostess] is glowing tonight?"*
	"I think this party is a glowing success, don't you?"
	"Does it look to you like this food is kind of glowing?"
H is for **Host**	*"So how do you know our host [or hostess]?"*
	"Look at Susan! She always was a natural-born hostess!"
	"Is there someone hosting this thing or did it just happen somehow?"
I is for **Ice**	*"Is it cold in here? My fingers are like ice."*
	"So many people drink wine now, no one ever has to worry about running out of ice."
	"Have you ever wondered who made up the saying 'break the ice'? And what does it really mean? What have you got afterwards except two or three pieces of ice?"
J is for **Jewelry**	*"What a beautiful ring (pair of earrings, watch, necklace)!"*

Letter	Sample lines
	"Is that an engagement (wedding) ring?"
	"If I had known it was going to be such a fancy party, I'd have worn my tiara."
K is for **Kill**	*"Isn't this cheesecake (paté, punch, dip) a killer?"*
	"Did any of you talk to those people over there? Boy, if looks could kill . . ."
	"My feet are killing me."
L is for **Laugh**	*"Tell me something funny; I could use a laugh."*
	"Do you think the best parties are the ones where you laugh the most?"
	"What this party needs is a laugh track."
M is for **Magic**	*"There's magic in the air tonight."*
	"I always wish I could do magic, so that when I met someone, I could pull a quarter out of their ear or something."
	"Wouldn't it be great if when the party was over, one could magically transport oneself home in bed?"
N is for **Noise**	*"Hey, how are ya? I hear you're making a big noise in the industry!"*
	"Do you think the noise level has any true correlation with the fun level?"

Letter	Sample lines
	"What do you suppose makes humans think the noise they make is any more important than the noise anything else makes?"
O is for **Old**	*"I can't believe how old I feel!"*
	"You know, you remind me of a very old friend of mine."
	"How old were you when you went to your first party?"
P is for **Practice** ...	*"I need practice talking to people I don't know."*
	"Don't you think they should throw a practice party before the real one?"
	"That food looks delicious. I think I'll practice for when I go off my diet."
Q is for **Quiche**	*"Was there any quiche?"*
	"Doesn't anyone make quiche anymore?"
	"Did you hear on the news that they've decided real men can eat quiche as long as they make it themselves and as long as they use egg substitute?"
R is for **Real Estate**...	*"Where do you live?"*
	"Isn't this a great (scary, funky, fun, popular) neighborhood?"

Letter	Sample lines
	"I'd love to own a house (apartment, condo, building, boat, convention hall) like this one."
S is for **Sun**	*"I feel like I've talked about everything under the sun."*
	"What a relief to talk to you. There's a guy here who thinks the sun rises and sets with him!"
	"You seem to have a fairly sunny disposition. Or am I about to get burnt?"
T is for **Toes**	*"Every time I come to one of these, someone steps on my toes."*
	"You look like someone who can really keep me on my toes!"
	"I'm this close to taking off my shoes and letting my toes roam free."
U is for **Utopia**	*"Would your Utopia have parties in it?"*
	"This party is a virtual Utopia!"
	"I have a friend who says Utopia is a place with no people. He obviously never met you."
V is for **Vocabulary**	*"Have you ever wondered just how many words there are in your vocabulary?"*
	"Tell me something unusual; I'm trying to improve my vocabulary."

Letter	Sample lines

"In this business, it's nice to meet someone with the same vocabulary."

W is for **Winner** ...

"Do you think of yourself as a winner?

"Hey, did you hear about [name of business associate]? She (he) sure turned out a winner!"

"Tonight I feel like life's just one big door prize, and I'm the winner."

X is for **Xerox** .....

"Keep in mind that you're not talking to the real me tonight; this is just a Xerox."

"I hope you'll bear with me. I've been repeating myself so much tonight I feel like a Xerox machine!"

"If we were to make a Xerox of this party, what position would you be in?"

Y is for **Yell** ....

"I glad we don't (I wish we didn't) have to yell."

"If I lose your interest, just yell."

"You know, sometimes at affairs like this one, I get the strangest urge to stand up on a chair and yell real loud."

Z is for **Zoo** ....

"Boy, what a zoo!"

"It was almost impossible to get here, it was such a zoo out there!"

> *"Have you ever thought that maybe we're really in some alien zoo and just don't know it?"*

Please note: the sample lines I've provided are merely *examples,* infused with my own sensibility. You can adapt the topics to your own conversational style, of course. Or, particularly if you're the kind of person who always thinks of great things to talk about before and after a party, but never during, you may prefer to substitute some of your *own* mingling topics—ones which are comfortable for you.

Also, this mingling "crib sheet" is purposely designed for observations or questions of a fairly nonpersonal nature. This is because, for the best mingling experience, you need to remain in control and, ideally, ready to move off to another group. Specific questions about personal life, while easy for most people to think of, usually commit you to an involved discourse with one person in the group. Using a little imagination will pay off in the long run!

Ten Tried-and-True Tricks of the Trade

• Playing a Game •

Here's a really fun way to keep things going but not dig too deeply. It takes a little courage, but you'll be pleasantly surprised at how well most people respond. I use this technique quite often, though I never realized it until a couple years ago, when I was spending a weekend with a friend in Stockbridge, Massachusetts. He and I had been arguing good-naturedly all day about whether my jacket was orange or red (he thought it was red; I *knew* it was orange). That night we went to a fairly large dance where I knew no one. My friend immediately melted into the crowd, leaving me to fend for myself. Never being much of one to stand alone in a corner, I marched right up to a group of people and entered it, using the Honest Approach. After the introductions were finished, there was that inevitable moment of silence; my intrusion had disturbed the conversational flow.

Suddenly, I had an idea. As if it were plaguing my mind, I asked the group at large, "What color would you call this jacket?" They were a little taken aback, but intrigued. They each answered in turn, and I noted that the two men said "red," and the woman, "orange." This lead to a quite interesting conversation about color perception and sex difference, and, as anyone knows, once you start talking about the differences between the sexes, you're home free.

The great thing about Playing a Game is it is such a fluid mingling technique. It facilitates bringing new members into the group ("Hey, come here, we want to ask you something!") as well as exiting a group ("I'll be back, I want some other opinions!"). Also, you get to know people by how they play the game, which is a more relaxing, easier—and sometimes more revealing—way to find out about someone. Game-playing is one of my absolutely most-reommended tactics; it epitomizes, I think, the true spirit of mingling!

Here are some sample game lines to explore. However, you'll definitely find that, once you use this device once or twice, you will begin to invent your own. Don't ever forget your primary goal (even if you are at a business function): Have fun!

- *"What color would you say this [——] is?"*
- *"Guess what my nickname was as a child?"* (*"Let me guess your childhood nickname."*)
- *"I'm into regional accents. Guess where I grew up?"* (*"Let me guess where you grew up."*)
- *"Close your eyes. Now tell me what I'm wearing."* (*"What color are my eyes?"*)
- *"Tell me three things about your company and I'll guess what company it is."*

• Party Favors: The Helpless Hannah Ploy •

Brace yourself, because this is probably going to offend some people. All I can say is that I've seen this method employed all my life, by children *and* adults, and it works. It's kind of a knock-down-drag-out way of mingling; but, while I've seen people doing it who, frankly, made me want to gag, I confess I've used it myself on occasion, with spectacular success. If done well, the Helpless Hannah Ploy can make you the star of the party.

Ready? Think of yourself as a damsel in distress or a knight in need, and the other guests as your rescuers. If you put people in the role of helping you, it: 1) gives them a purpose, 2) flatters them, 3) leaves you in control and 4) most important, gives you something to say.

My favorite version of this technique is getting someone to "protect me" from someone else. For example, after my opening, I'll say, "Listen. There's someone here I'm desperately trying to avoid—I can't tell you who it is—but you'd be doing me a big favor if when you see me doing this," and I show them some subtle hand or eye signal, "you'd just come over and check up on me if you can." Naturally, people want to know who it is and why I am avoiding them. I won't be able to tell them, of course, having made the whole thing up, but it makes for great conversation. Also, usually what happens is that the person or people will keep checking up on me to see if I need protection even if I don't give the signal (which I usually don't). If you tell a few different sets of people this story, you can get a big rush all evening, and everyone will wonder what your secret power is.

Another—often more subtle—way to play Helpless Hannah is to ask as many people as you can to help you obtain *information*. You can say to person X that you heard an important business contact was going to be present, and would X mind letting you know when the contact arrives. If X doesn't know the contact, you can still ask X to keep her ears open for anyone who does. You can mention to person Y that later on in the evening, you will need a ride home, and if Y should happen to meet anyone who he knows is going in your direction, to please let you know. When introduced to person Z, you can ask him for yet a different piece of information or use one of the ones you used before.

It doesn't matter what information you request. The important part of this gambit is that when X, Y, or Z says he doesn't have the answer to your question, you say, "Well, do me a favor and let me know if you *do* find out." That way, if you query enough people, some of them will return throughout the evening to report to you. Getting people involved with you in this manner is your insurance against ever being a wallflower.

The other, more Scarlett O'Hara form of the Helpless Hannah is asking people to get you *things*. You'll need to invent a reason you can't get the thing yourself, which can be tricky and can occasionally backfire, but if you are able to pull it off, this can serve an additional purpose: getting rid of somebody. Here's how it works.

Betty has just begun to talk to John and Tom. From the responses to the Sophistication Test she has just used ("How did you get here?") she senses Tom is more interesting than John. The conversation has died down now and all three people are beginning to get that furtive look signalling the early stages of minglephobia, until Betty says to John, "Would you mind doing me a big favor and getting me a glass of wine? There's someone over there near the bar I'd really rather not talk to." John has no choice, really, but to acquiesce. So off he goes, leaving Betty with the more interesting Tom, at least for the moment.

You can use many other excuses to play Helpless Hannah. You can say you have to wait near the phone; you can say you don't want to lose your place in line for food or for the powder room. But whatever reason you give, be nice, act sincere, and always be very grateful if and when the person returns with the requested item. If you have several people protecting you, several people getting you information, and another bunch of people bringing you things, it can really liven up your mingling experience. People will be coming up to you constantly, giving you things, asking if you're okay, and trying to find out the identity of the mysterious person you're avoiding. You can end up with an absolute throng around you. People will wonder whether you are wearing some irresistible cologne, or whether you're some kind of underground celebrity!

There are some serious dangers involved with the Helpless Hannah approach that I'm sure are fairly obvious. Don't overdo the avoiding line—people will think you are paranoid or a snob—and never, never indicate an actual guest as the object of your avoidance (even if it's true). I did this once, in an effort to make my Helpless Hannah a little more believable. After asking for protection, I pointed a finger surreptitiously at the back of a man standing at the bar. To my horror, the woman I had been talking to turned a cold eye on me and said with suspicion, *"That's my husband!"*

• Room with a View •

If you are at a fairly large party, you might want to try this device, which is a little cowardly but still perfectly acceptable. Suppose you are slightly depressed and feeling very non-witty, and you have just begun to talk to either one or two people (this strategy works best in a small group).

What you do is point out (subtly, please!) someone else at the party, preferably someone across the room, and make an observation. People *love* to talk about other people, and this way you can have a very nonthreatening verbal exchange, and find out a little about whom you're talking to before you decide to enter into more personal territory. Here are some lines you might try:

- *"Did you see that woman over there? Isn't that the wildest hat you've ever seen?"*

- *"Look at old J.B. I've never seen him look so happy, have you?"*

43

- *"See that man over by the door? Do you know who he is? I think I've met him somewhere, but I can't remember."*

- *"Have you talked to that person over there? Is she a friend of yours? I found her very interesting (funny, mysterious, etc.)."*

The lines you use, of course, will depend on what you can notice about people at a specific party. If you're at a Halloween party you can have a field day! **Warning:** I am *not* condoning vicious gossip. It is vital to remember that you are not, under any circumstances, to say anything nasty about the object of your voyeurism. Doing so can get you into more hot water than I have space to talk about here.

• Using Clichés •

Just because I am overly fond of clichés myself doesn't mean that I necessarily recommend their use for others. But there actually is a good way, in conversations, to use clichés effectively.

Irony is the key. The following lines, executed with enough irony, sarcasm, or just plain playfulness, can become your staples:

"Haven't I seen you somewhere before?"

"Do you come here often?"

"My name's Robert but my friends call me Robbie."

"Are you having a good time?"

"Is that a gun in your pocket or are you just glad to see me?"

"What's your sign?"

"We've got to stop meeting like this."

Exaggerated, these standards can work as openers or as second or third lines (better irony results if they are *not* first lines), and they also serve as a sort of Sophistication Test. Best of all, they're easy to remember!

• Talking Shop •

If you are at party connected to an official business function, such as your industry's annual convention, the most obvious thing to talk about is work. It's something you *know* you have in common with everyone there, so it's the one area you know has to elicit some response. Besides, people feel that they are more or less expected to be talking about work at work-related affairs. Shop talk is fine; however, there are still some dos and don'ts to keep in mind:

DOs

- Ask after family (especially kids).

- Talk about vacation plans (yours or theirs).

- Talk about the economy and how it affects your industry.

- Ask about a specific project you know about.

- Congratulate someone on a promotion.

- Ask what big or interesting projects they're working on at the moment.

- Talk about TV, sports, movies, plays, books, or new restaurants.

DON'Ts

- Gossip about people; not unless you know the person to whom you are gossiping pretty well, or unless the gossip is *so* juicy it has become an irresistible mingler's tool.

- Ask people how much they make.

- Drink too much.

- Tell people you hate your job, or your superiors or colleagues.

- Talk only with people from your own company or department.

- Talk about a work problem that involves people who are at the party.

• Name-Tag Tips •

I went through a period in my life when I refused to wear the sticky, annoying labels we are all encouraged to don at many business, pseudo-business, alumnae, or association affairs. After all, if you're wearing a bright blue or red tag which announces "HELLO MY NAME IS————," you can feel kind of dumb *saying* it as well; it's almost as if you're reading your name tag aloud to the other person. I always used to have this nightmarish fantasy that someone would yell back at me, *"Hey I can read stupid!"*

I've mellowed on the subject of name tags since then. Now I believe you should wear them if they are provided—with the exception of the ones that pin on. (Call me fussy, but I don't think anyone should be asked to put holes in their clothing in the name of socializing, unless they're wearing burlap or something disposable.) Even though name tags are a silly mingling crutch, I have found that it is better to go ahead and wear them, if for no other reason than if you don't, it makes the people who *are* wearing them feel dorky. Also—you never know—someone at the party may have been told to talk to you because you're fabulous or brilliant, and that person may be darting in and out of clusters of people, reading tags and hoping to find you. If you are not wearing a name tag, you could miss the best conversation of your life.

But if you are bored by the prospect of conventional name-tag practice, here are some suggestions to liven things up:

- **Wear it in an interesting place.** People are doing this more and more. I've seen tags on lapels (sideways), purses or briefcases, hats, the lower part of a jacket—even sleeves. Women often choose an alternative to the chest because they feel uncomfortable having people look pointedly at that part of the body. I say as long as you have chosen to wear a name tag, you may as well get the most out of it conversationally. And if your tag is in an interesting—even original—place, it can be a real ice-breaker.

- **Write something else instead of your name.** This is admittedly kind of silly, but what's wrong with silly? You could write something like: "Guess." or "You'd never be able to pronounce it." or "I've got amnesia." or maybe "Don't you hate name tags?" I've even heard of taping on a bar code in place of a name. You'd be surprised how many people enjoy seeing something out of the ordinary. **Warning:** Don't go too far. Never, never write something that is crude or impolite in any way (this includes remarks that are sexist, racist, etc.). If you have to ask yourself "Is this offensive?" don't use it.

- **Write your name and draw an arrow pointing toward your face.** This is a little cutesy, but some people like cutesy.

- **Use punctuation.** The obvious one is an exclamation mark. A question mark may be a good choice for a very intellectual party. Underlining can be distinctive yet conservative. And for the serious business gathering: your last name first, then a comma, then your first name; better still—your first name underneath (in parentheses).

- **Write illegibly.** Scrawl or scratch your name so that no one can possibly decipher it. This can serve as an interesting test to see who will admit they can't read it and who won't. And when someone does comment on it, you can have some conversation starters ready, such as: "It's my own personal protest against name tags," or "I always wanted to be a doctor but I never got past Bad Handwriting 101."

- **Use a fictitious name.** This is reminiscent of the Lucky Star fantasy. It's much easier to do, but takes more guts because someone can catch you. However, if you're bored with the same old you or sick of being shy, put someone else's name down, and try a bold new conversational style! If you flop, no one will ever know it was you. **Caution:** Obviously, you have to possess a certain recklessness to try this. You can't get away with it if people at the party know you, and it's not a great idea if you are going to do business with them face-to-face in the future. Also, you must not use the name of someone else you *know;* that would be dangerous, stupid, and possibly illegal. But you could try what my

47

friend Henry does without fail at every name-tag function: He writes, in very small letters, the name of a celebrity. His favorites are Rock Hudson, Mickey Mouse, and Pat Paulsen. It's a bit obnoxious, but he manages to get away with it. Remember, most people *hate* name tags.

Whether or not you choose to employ any of the above un-subtle name-tag tricks, there are a couple of things to keep in mind when mingling among name-tag wearers.

If you are going with the straight name-tag approach, be sure to write clearly in large letters so that people don't have to stick their faces in your chest to read your name. Also, it's best not to look at a person's tag until you have approached him or the group he is in. It's very rude to be seen checking out the tags of everyone in the room without joining a group, *unless* you can appear to be looking for someone specific. Therefore, if you *do* glance at people's tags while you pass by, do not make eye contact with any of them. If you do, it's as if you are saying, "I don't like your name, I don't like your face; I'm going to look elsewhere for conversational partners." Also, when you enter into a conversation with someone, it's best to be definite with regard to the tag; either look at it and comment on it, or *don't* look at it (at least not so they notice).

A great name-tag trick is to glance quickly at the tag without letting the wearer see you. Then wait a few minutes and slip the wearer's name into the conversation as if you're old chums ("Well, Bob . . .") This simple trick, when done well, seems to impress most people. And if they do catch you looking at their tag, the worst that can happen is that you *don't* impress them, particularly.

One last piece of advice on this subject: Be sure you stick the tag on right-side up. There's a famous story about a guy who had just arrived from Hong Kong and, in his jet-lagged state, affixed his tag to his jacket upside-down. All night long people kept saying to him, "Pardon me, but did you know you were upside-down?" Finally he couldn't take it any longer, and when the next person said to him that he was upside-down, he snapped, "I can't believe you all still believe that over here!"

• About Eye Contact •

When it comes to being a good mingler, subject matter isn't everything. The wittiest line, if it's delivered while you're looking at the floor or someone's crotch, is worthless. Here are a few tried-and-true tips about how your eyes—the most important mingling asset you have—should behave.

1. **Look straight at anyone who is speaking to you.** I mean this literally; that is, look into the person's eyes during those periods when sound is actually coming out of that person's mouth. Eyes are extremely powerful, and as long as you are looking at the other person, you can be in La-La Land and still appear to be listening.

2. **Use the time when you are speaking to look away.** Certainly, if you are having a very intense discussion, you may be too spellbound to want to do this, and that's okay. But it's a fact of human communication that while you are speaking, you can turn your eyes anywhere else in the room and still seem totally involved in the present conversation. This works as long as, when the other person resumes speaking, you immediately make eye contact with them again. This really works, although it seems to surprise people whenever I mention it. **Note:** With close friends, the rules of eye contact change. Both people can stare at the ceiling and the conversation still works.

I encourage you to practice your eye-roaming because it is essential, if you want to become an expert mingler, to be aware of what is happening around you. First, your escape will be a lot easier if you know where you want to escape *to,* and for that you have to scope out the room.

49

Secondly, there are techniques you may want to slide into at a moment's notice—the Helpless Hannah, a Room with a View—which necessitate keen peripheral vision.

3. **Use your eyes for emphasis.** If you learn to use your eyes well, it's almost as good as having a million-dollar smile. Many people, in their frenzy to keep up a dialogue, forget that the eyes are the true center of communication. You can use eye contact to pick someone out of a group and let him know you want to talk to him one on one. You can use your eyes, along with a very slight nod, to point out something in the room. You can use eye expressions instead of words, either because words fail you or just because your eyes can say it better: Roll your eyes ("Oh, I *know!*"), shut your eyes (Oh, how horrible!"), blink your eyes fast ("I'm trying to take this in, but it's all very strange"), or raise your eyebrows ("Oh, really?"). I admit to being one of those enviable people who can raise one eyebrow, a very dramatic gesture and very effective (Oh, *come on* now!"). Practice these eye expressions in the mirror; they can not only save you when you don't know what to say, but also add to your general conversational charm.

• The Dot-Dot-Dot Plot •

I have used, and needed, this trick at every party I have ever attended. I rely on this technique because, I'm embarrassed to confess, I have an extremely short attention span and if I am not constantly entertained, my mind tends to wander. This can be *very* awkward at a party. Suddenly I'll find that someone has been talking to me and I have no idea what she has been talking about. And now she's *stopped* talking and I am expected to respond. The feeling of panic is exactly like getting called on in class when you've been daydreaming. As an adult, getting caught not paying attention at a party when someone is speaking directly to you is a *serious* mingling faux pas. I still experience that split-second rush of adrenaline when

50

it happens. But then I remember: Have no fear, the Dot-dot-dot Plot is here.

When you "come to" in this situation, you almost always are aware of the last few words the person has said. It's just that without any other clues, you're lost. What you can do is use those few words any way you can, and then employ the all-important, all-powerful pause. They are not going to suspect you haven't been listening (unless you tell them), *if you have maintained eye contact*. Keep in mind that everyone is busy thinking about how they themselves are performing. So as long as you give them a "You mean . . ." or a "So what you're saying, really, is . . ." or "I don't know that much about it, but. . . ," they'll go right on talking.

I promise that you are going to be surprised at how well this works. It's scary the first time you try it; it sort of feels like stepping out into thin air, but when you find out how successful and powerful the pause is, you'll be astounded. One of the most popular "closing" techniques taught at sales seminars is something called the "Pause Close." It's based on the same principle as the Dot-dot-dot Plot: Human beings are very uncomfortable with pauses and will automatically do anything to end them. The Dot-dot-dot Plot is really very simple to use; in a way, it is just a glorified version of "Uh-huh." Note: The more you are able to work the last few words you may have heard into your delivery, the more convincing it will be. Here are ten Dot-dot-dot Plot lines you can use.

"You mean . . ."

"So what you're saying is . . ."

"I don't know much about that kind of thing . . ."

"You can say that again . . ."

"I'll say . . ."

"Wow . . ."

"You're kidding . . ."

51

"Really? . . ."

"You can't be serious . . ."

"Amazing . . ."

• The Funny Thing About Humor •

The funny thing about humor is how often people try to be funny and how rarely they are. A lot of people see a bright, gaily laughing group and think laughter must be the key to success and therefore they've got to be funny. But there's nothing worse than humor badly executed while mingling. Please don't let this happen to you:

"Hiya stranger!! Hee Hee! Want to hear a funny story? Ha Ha! This is so funny, it's going to kill you!! Hee hee! A man walks up to a . . . this is so funny, just wait . . . a man walks up to a bar . . . ha ha . . . I mean, a woman walks up to a bar, no a woman walks *into* a bar, hee hee, . . . this is so great . . . wait . . . hey, wait a minute, where are you going?"

Painful? An extreme case, I admit. But you'd be surprised how many people turn to humor when they shouldn't, especially when they are nervous. It's so tempting; humor *is* risky, but when it works, the rewards are great. I'm not about to try and teach anyone how to be funny. Humor is a very individual thing, and its success or failure depends as much on the climate as grape vines do. But here are a few basic guidelines:

1. **Don't try to be funny.** If you're trying too hard, it won't be funny. Be aware that you may try overly hard when you are feeling insecure.

2. **Don't tell jokes.** Unless you enter a group that is into joke-telling, or the joke you have to tell is a proven success *and* is relevant to the day's events (or the party itself), it is

best to stay away from joke-telling. There are few things worse than when your joke bombs in front of strangers (ask any comic).

3. **Don't announce in advance that your personal anecdote is going to be funny.**

4. **Don't make your stories inordinately long.**

5. **Don't touch people to encourage them to laugh.**

6. **Don't laugh too much yourself.** In fact, it's best not to laugh at all, at least not until they do. A big smile is enough.

7. **Don't make fun of other people.** If you must make fun of someone to get a laugh, let it be yourself.

8. **Don't be a punster. Most people hate puns. If you can't manage to hold back a pun, be prepared for groans!**

• How to Handle the Joker in Every Deck. •

You may be thinking at this point, "What do I do when I'm up against a humor nitwit myself?" It's a good question, because there's usually one at every party. Besides escape, which is the subject of the next chapter, there are a couple of defensive techniques that will help. If it's a joke-telling joker, you can always say, "Oh, yes, that's a funny one, I've heard it already" either to shut him up or to explain why you're not laughing. Or before they get going, smile politely and say, "Jokes are a waste of time on me, I'm afraid. I'm just not a joke person."

Let's say you are up against someone who seems to thrive on saying stupid things and then laughing at them. If you choose to stay or for some reason cannot escape, you're going to have to decide whether to humor the idiot or try to squelch him. You can always try a line my parents used on me when I was a kid: "Have you taken silly pills or something?" Or just smile vaguely until he gets the point that you don't think he's funny.

In the end, we have to forgive even the worst jokers. They mean well, after all, and may simply be unsure of themselves; so always try to be kind.

On the other hand, if your tolerance is low and you are starting to feel like kicking some joker, it may be time to . . . bail out and move on!

·4·

THE GREAT ESCAPE:
Bailing Out
and Moving On

W hen I speak of escaping, I do not mean leaving the social event itself. I'm talking about something much more difficult: how to remove yourself, as gracefully as possible, from a conversation. As almost everyone knows, getting *into* a conversation may be hard, but getting *out* is often much harder.

A friend of mine told me a story that positively made my skin crawl. He had attended a party—a business function—even though he had just hurt his back and was in a fair amount of pain. Though he had gone to the affair with hopes of forgetting his troubles, his physical discomfort caused him to bring up the subject of his injury with a fellow guest.

"You hurt your back?" the man said excitedly. "Boy, are you in for it now! You're going to have trouble with that now for the rest of your life! Let me tell you . . ."

Realizing his mistake in introducing this literally painful topic, my friend tried weakly to change the subject, even going so far as to say that he really wasn't in the mood to talk about it, thank you. But the man would not stop.

". . . You know what you've got in store for you? What are you, about thirty? Well, it's all downhill from here. Listen, all my friends have chronic back pain. You'll never be the same again, I'm telling you. . . ."

Helplessly, my friend tried to edge away, but the man had found his prey; he went right along with him. It was a most unpleasant experience and went on for what seemed an eternity. My friend swore off parties for a month after that.

I have heard hundreds of similar stories, though most of them are not quite so terrible. Most of the time it is simply a question of being stuck in a conversation when you would rather be talking to someone else. The key to having a good time at parties is being in control of whom you're talking to, and for how long.

Personally, I find that extricating myself from a person or small group takes more planning and effort than entering even the toughest of groups. In fact, it can be so difficult to get away from some people, that many minglers just give up and settle in, resigned to the fact that they are probably going to be with this person all evening. Often it may seem easier to stay put than to make the effort to move, especially if the current conversation isn't *too* dreadful. I even know one man who actually *tries* to get stuck; he seeks out another person at the party who shares his desire to stay in one place, with one person, the whole night, so that he won't have to worry about entering or exiting conversations.

Don't take the easy way out. The term *mingling* implies talking to *a lot* of people; if you remain in one place with no clue (or no inclination) as to how to move on, you're not mingling, no matter how great a conversation you are having. Naturally, if you discover the love of your life or the most fascinating person in the universe (or both, if you're lucky!), you may decide to stop moving around and stay where you are. That's okay, of course. But it isn't mingling! Mingling means circulating. And to circulate successfully, you have to know *when* to make your move, and *how*.

WHEN TO MOVE

• Boredom and Other Discomforts •

The most obvious reason to move on is your own misery. Everyone has a personal tale of excruciating agony, that time they were hopelessly stuck with Mr. Obnoxious or Ms. Boring of the century. Usually a kind of inner panic sets in, and

you try to talk yourself through it. ("Okay, I'm going to get out of this . . . Oh, my God, this is terrible . . . Why doesn't he just shut up for one second . . . Okay, I can get out of this somehow . . ."), while on the outside, you smile with a glassy stare (the Glaze-out) and act as if you are listening. There's never any question about it in these cases. You need to get out as quickly, as permanently, and as gracefully as you can, whether you are imprisoned by a bore, a drunk, a talkaholic, a wolf, a vamp, a joker, or just someone who wants you to get them a job.

• Saving Face •

The great thing about large parties is that if you do happen to make a faux pas, make a joke that no one else thinks is funny, or otherwise embarrass or humiliate yourself, you can leave the witnesses behind and start over somewhere else with a fresh slate. Just forget your failure and try again with someone new.

• The Case of the Vanishing Group •

This can be frightening. Usually it begins without your even being aware of it; suddenly you notice there are fewer people in the group you have been working. And the smaller the group gets, the harder it is going to be for you to get out yourself. Also, in the case of the vanishing group, there is usually a reason for its sudden shrinkage; namely, there's one person in the group who is undesirable in some way. If you don't watch out, you're going to be the last one left, trapped with him or her. It's very much like a game of musical chairs, except that in this case you don't have to depend on luck to win. Keep your eye out for the vanishing group, and leave before it's too late!

• Time's Up •

Optimum mingling time is five to twenty minutes per person or group, and *never* more than a half hour. You may be having a wonderful time, but you must move on. I know it's hard to leave when you're having fun, but remember, you are there to meet people, as many as you can. Tell yourself that you can come back to this person after you've met ten more people. Or get the person's card and ask him or her if you can get together one on one another time. Take the good energy generated from the successful communication and inject it into your next encounter!

Warning: Overzealous minglers may, on the other hand, move too quickly. I must plead guilty to doing this sometimes; I get so into the motion of mingling, the excitement of interaction that I sometimes realize I am spending only thirty or forty seconds in one place. And that is definitely not enough time to do anything but leave a "Who was that masked man?" feeling behind.

THE ETIQUETTE OF ESCAPE

• Knowing Where You're Headed •

Before employing any of the escape techniques described in this chapter, it's essential that you have a clear idea about where you are going next. Ideally, your next target will be a person or group, but you can also set your sights on a place (the bathroom, the bar, the food table). Many of the following escape lines include a mention of where you are headed, and of course you must at least pretend to do whatever you announce you are going off to do. But even if you decide you just want to walk around, be sure to plan your general route or direction in advance. For one thing, if there is any time other people may be watching you (which, as I pointed out in Chapter 1, isn't likely), it's when you are leaving and entering cliques of people. Movement catches the eye, and if you break away from the group and then are uncertain where to go next, you could end up looking lost and unwanted. The longer you are alone, not attached to any group, the more alienated you can feel, until you end up wondering why you left your last conversation anyway and how you can get back in. More important, if you don't appear to have a definite destination, the people you've just left could feel insulted, realizing that you would rather be alone than talk to them.

Always remember: The best time to scope out the room is when *you* are talking, especially if you are with only one or two other people. When someone is talking to *you,* you must maintain eye contact. However, if you are in a larger group, you can surreptitiously scan when you know the attention isn't focused on you. Try not to be caught looking off across the room, obviously wishing you were somewhere else.

• The Five Laws of Survival •

Mingling has its very own set of rules, many of which are different from the generally accepted standards of etiquette à la Amy Vanderbilt. Since it is during escape maneuvers that your sense of courtesy and graciousness will come in direct conflict with your instinct for survival, here are five rules to govern your exit behavior as a mingler, rules that you will find especially helpful to remember as you get ready to break away.

1. **It's okay to tell a lie.** That's right. Forget all that stuff you learned in school about George Washington and the cherry tree. George was probably terrible at parties. Lying for the purpose of mingling well is most assuredly in the white lie category. Anyway, it's essential for most exit techniques.

2. **No one knows what you are really thinking.** Even psychics can't read your exact thoughts. For the most part, other people know only what you tell them and what you show them.

3. **The other person is thinking primarily about himself.** It helps to remember this if you are nervous about someone seeing through your act, whatever it is.

4. **It's better to escape from someone than have someone escape from you.** Law number four is a good motivator if you tend to procrastinate too much while preparing to escape; there's nothing much worse at a party than being left standing by yourself.

5. **Change equals movement; movement equals change.** This is the most profound law and applies to all aspects of

mingling (as well as all aspects of life, if you want to get philosophical). The only real crime in mingling is stasis.

THE GETAWAY: NINE EXIT MANEUVERS

• The Honest Approach in Reverse •

When I talk about "honesty" in mingling, I'm not usually talking about truthfulness (which has nothing much to do with mingling) so much as a kind of straightforwardness. If you're like me and tend to be direct, you may want to use this exit technique whenever possible. It works only if you have been with one person or the same set of people for a respectable amount of time (ten minutes or so). As sincerely as possible, say something like: "Well, as enjoyable as this is, I think it's time to mingle," or "Well, I don't want to monopolize your time, and anyway I think we're supposed to mingle at this thing." Or you can use a version of one of the opening lines from page 22: "Excuse me, but I really must go practice my mingling!" This maneuver constitutes a strong, definite form of exit; it announces your intention to leave in a manner that is not open to negotiation, and at the same time it offers an excuse that is more honest, at least, than many of the excuses people usually use to escape. It is, in fact, the most truthful line you can employ without admitting straight out that you find the prospect of continued interaction with them unappealing.

Note: This exit technique works even better when it is coupled with the Honest Approach entrance. If your opening line has already established you as an guileless person and an enthusiastic mingler, people are going to buy this exit line much more easily.

• The Fade-out •

This one needs very little explanation; it is something that almost everyone who has ever attended a large party has done. It is usable only when you're not too involved in conversation—and therefore you are not really trapped—and you simply want to move away as unobtrusively as possible.

As you may guess, the directions for the Fade-out are the exact opposite of those for the Fade-in technique (see page 17). Wait until no one is talking to you or looking at you too closely, and then . . . slowly start to back away. Watch and listen carefully as you begin your disappearing act, in case the conversation should happen to turn back to you in mid-fade. When you feel you are far enough away from the group to be unnoticed, make tracks!

Two warnings: You must not try this unless you are in a cluster of four (counting yourself) or more. Otherwise, you can be caught during Fade-out, and that can be extremely awkward. Also, if you *are* caught—and this can happen even while leaving a large group—you need to switch immediately into another escape tactic. So have one ready, just in case.

• The Changing of the Guard •

This well-known exit maneuver was one I had actually forgotten about until one night I attended a cocktail party on Manhattan's Upper East Side. I had set my mingling sights on a dashing-looking man I had met earlier during the party. He was standing in a group with two other people. I used the Fade-in (with just a smidge of the Touchy-Feely Mingle, something I'll talk about later), addressing my first remark to the man who was my primary target. The *second* I was "in," the other two guests took off, but fast! I was stunned by the sudden realization that my entrance had given them a way out and that this admittedly passive escape technique is used all the time, by practically everyone. I was so floored that my mouth fell open, and I just stood there like an idiot, staring at the disappearing duo.

This exit method works because of law number five: Change equals movement; movement equals change. As soon as a new person, or a new energy, enters the circle, a readjustment of some kind—no matter how subtle—automatically occurs. It's as though the new person has kicked up psychic dust, and while everyone is waiting for the dust to settle, people can slip away. I also call this strategy "the Substitution Illusion" because the person exiting is using the illusion that because a new person is taking his place, it's okay for him (the exiter) to go now. It's a fascinating aspect of mingling, and makes for a totally facile escape. The drawback is obvious: To use the Changing of the Guard, you have to wait until someone new arrives. And it could be a very long wait.

• The Smooth Escape •

When you can pull this off, it makes you feel great—like a champion of minglers. It does however, take a little finesse. What the Smooth Escape has going for it is that it works in drastic situations and, when done well, it's so subtle and natural that no one realizes they've just been handled.

The three steps of the Smooth Escape are: 1) Take control of the conversation. 2) change the subject. 3) exit gracefully.

Easier said than done, I know. But here's an example.

Say you started out talking to a circle of four or five people but, one by one, they have peeled off until you are left alone with Joe Obnoxious, who is pressed up against you and is talking nonstop about his job as a computer salesman. Having failed to detect the Case of the Vanishing Group in time, you are now in one of the most challenging spots a mingler can be in. Don't despair. You *can* get out of this. But take a deep breath and concentrate, because you are going to need to be more alert for the Smooth Escape than you obviously have been so far.

The first thing you must do is focus totally on what Joe is saying, so that you will be able to seize the slightest opportunity to wrest control of the dialogue. For example, as he is saying, ". . . so my real problem has been in this economic climate, that people are demanding more flexible software systems but aren't interested in buying the actual components . . ." you can break in with "By 'actual components' do

63

you mean the keyboard, the disk drive, the monitor?" (You've *taken control*).

"Why . . . sort of . . . I mean the components are . . ." Joe will start to say. Interrupt him again with something like, "Because I really need a new system—you just wouldn't believe the antique I'm using now—it's a clunky word processor from the early eighties and I've had it *forever!* Can you believe how long ago the early eighties seem to us now?" (You've *changed the subject*.) While Joe is busy trying to switch gears to follow you, keep talking. "It seems like only yesterday that Ronald Reagan was elected for the first time." At this point, while you are still speaking, focus on something across the room, as if something irresistible has caught your attention, touch Joe Obnoxious's arm gently and say, "Excuse me, won't you?" Then move quickly away.

The Smooth Escape can be a bit tricky, but keep the following in mind: If you act as if the conversation has been brought to its natural close, and that you've had a lovely time talking to Mr. Obnoxious but the dance is over now, your behavior won't come off as rude. And don't forget, Mr. Obnoxious has probably been run out on at parties most of his life. To him, it may be normal. The important thing to remember is that when you are really stuck with someone, the only way to get away is to take control of the situation.

• Shake and Break •

This escape route also involves taking control, but you have to have just the right circumstances to execute it properly. (This is a good one to practice on a nerd before trying it out for real.) Use it only at a very large party, preferably a business party, when you are sure you are not going to mingle again with the same person or cluster. In other words, you have to be making your way through a large room of people, intending to leave when you have covered everyone; or, you have to have a *very* good memory and avoid your Shake-and-Break victims for the rest of the night.

64

How it's done: Suppose you are up against a talker like Mr. Obnoxious. As you are smiling at him and responding facially to what he is saying, stick your hand out until he instinctively takes it, or just grab his hand (this won't work if he's got his hands in his pockets). Shake it until he either stops speaking or at least slows down; then smile warmly, and tell him "It's been so nice meeting [talking with] you!" Then turn and walk away. In the opposite situation, where you are trapped with Mr. Awkward Silences, the Shake-and-Break technique is even easier, as you will not have to interrupt the flow of conversation. Just shake . . . and break!

• The Human Sacrifice •

Most people are too embarrassed to admit that they use this device to escape from undesirable mingling partners, but I see it done at almost every gathering I attend. It's a clever maneuver because it poses as a social grace. The only prerequisite is that you know at least one other person at the party.

Imagine you are engaged in what seems to be an inescapable discourse with Betsy Boring. You are either alone with Betsy, or one other person is with you, a very quiet person—not much help in this situation (in other words, you can't fade out while the two of them are talking. And Betsy is talking to *you*). While nodding enthusiastically to what she is saying, reach out and snare someone you either know or with whom you've had a solid conversation, and pull that person into the group. Introduce the new person to Betsy in a way that suggests that you are doing them both a favor, that they have a lot in common or will like each other enormously. Here's the key: *As soon as their eyes meet,* either do a fast fade or leave in a more overt manner, but get out quickly.

This trick works for the same reason the Changing of the Guard works: you've changed the cast of characters; you've brought in a replacement. Of course, the more sophisticated minglers will know exactly what you're doing. In fact, I've been used as a sacrifice many times; I can spot the maneuver as soon as I'm summoned, but there's not much to do except to find another sacrifice as soon as you can or escape in some other manner. But obvious or not, the Human Sacrifice is still a perfectly acceptable move. All's fair in love and mingling!

Warning: If you wait until a candidate for the Human Sacrifice passes by, you could be there with Ms. Boring till the end of time, or the end of the party, whichever comes first. It's easiest if someone does pass right by you, of course, but there are many more active versions of this ploy. You can take Ms. Boring (if you're alone with her) by the arm and, while conversing, gently lead her over to another person or group. If she won't budge, you can interrupt her and say, "Do you mind if we join my friend over there?" Or even "Let's go get some food" **Note:** this is different than the Buffet Bye-Bye, below. Once over by the food, or anywhere close to other people, you can even use a stranger for your Human Sacrifice, if you can just lure someone new into the conversation and then skidaddle. It's like having gum on your shoe, you can't get it off until you find something to scrape it off on.

• Escape by Mutual Consent •

In all likelihood, this won't happen to you very often. When it does, it will result in great relief and maybe a little embarrassment.

Sometimes two people who end up talking to each other will realize at more or less the same moment that they are in a bad marriage, mingling wise. You will simply look at the other person and be able to tell that he or she feels exactly the way you do; the dialogue between you is either played out, or you were mismatched in the first place. Usually one of you will smile sheepishly and say, "Well . . ." and the other will respond, "Well, it's been nice to . . ." and then the first one will say "Good to talk to you!" And with a respectful nod or even a handshake, you'll turn away from each other at the same time and head off happily toward your next encounter. It's rare that such a clean and easy "divorce" occurs, but it does happen.

• The Buffet Bye-Bye and Other Handy Excuses •

Without question, this is the most commonly used escape technique, especially among men (there are, in fact, some extremely fascinating mingling differences between the sexes). What you do here is wait for any sort of lull in the conversation, then deliver any of the following excuses:

"I've got to get some food."

"I have to get something to drink."

"I have to powder my nose." (Yes, I still use this euphemism, just for fun.) Cutesy cat-lover's version: "I have to visit the sandbox."

"Excuse me, I must find my husband [wife, boyfriend, fiancé]."

"Pardon me, but I simply must sit down!"

"Excuse me, I promised to help the host (hostess)." (the Good Samaritan).

"Do you have the time? . . . Really? Oh, excuse me, I must make a phone call." (This excuse is known as the Telephone Line).

In spite of the ease with which these familiar excuses can roll off your tongue and their popularity among most party-goers, I myself do not use the Buffet Bye-Bye more than is absolutely necessary. The reason is that you must actually *do* what it is you have said you will do, even if you don't feel like it, and even if you are sure your Buffet Bye-Bye escape victim isn't looking. This can really cut into your party fun. You can end up overeating, for example, or drinking too much, or—worse still—*standing in line for the bathroom when you don't need to go.*

The other danger with this technique is that the person from whom you are trying to escape will offer to go *with* you to the food table, the bar, the couch, or even the bathroom.

There's nothing for you to do in that case but agree cheerfully and hope you can shake them off at the specified location. Also, depending on the situation and how old-fashioned you are, you may feel rude unless you offer to get the other person, or even the whole group, a drink, if you use thirst as an excuse. And *never,* under any circumstances, is it acceptable to promise someone to fetch them a drink and then not come back, though I know people who will deliver the offered drink quickly and then move on. But it's not easy to do this smoothly.

My recommended choice of excuses may surprise you: It's the Telephone Line. The reason is twofold. For one thing, the telephone is one place no one (well, *hardly* anyone) will ever follow you. It is implied, just by the statement that you have to make a call, that you are taking care of something personal. You must, of course, actually make a call. You can call the weather or the time, or even your own machine—I like this last option the most because then when I get home I have my own fake message waiting for me, and I get a kick out of remembering the harmless charade.

The Telephone Line also can double as an exit from the party itself, should you find that you are desperate to leave before it is particularly polite to do so. If you do want to leave the party, you can fabricate any number of believable—even intriguing—stories about whom you called and why you have to leave. Or you can just be mysterious and say cryptically, "I'm sorry—I must leave!" and dash out in a flurry.

• The Counterfeit Search •

Try this technique at your next party and I guarantee you will have enormous fun with it. It takes a little body language, specifically use of the eyes.

It's especially easy to flow into this exit ploy if you are bored by the person who is talking to you. Your attention is probably already drifting, and you are going to be using any time you can to look around the room—either because you are scoping out your next conversational target or simply because you're bored. Try to follow the rule about scanning the room only while you are speaking; however, this is one time it may be necessary to let your eyes rove a bit *while* the other person is speaking to you. If you remember to look at him intermittently you can get away with it. The trick is to give the impression that something inescapable is beginning to pull your attention away from your current conversational clique—totally against your will. To complete the maneuver, suddenly focus your eyes on someone (real or imagined) across the room and exclaim, "Oh!" Look embarrassed and confused for a moment, as if you didn't really mean to say that out loud. Then smile apologetically and say something like, "I'm sorry, but there's a person over there I've been looking for since I arrived," or "Excuse me, will you, I just spotted someone I haven't seen for two years!" Or, at a business function: "Pardon me, but I just noticed a person across the room my boss particularly instructed me to talk to."

The Counterfeit Search can be a little abrupt, but if you put enough energy into making it look sincere, it's one of the quickest ways to exit. In fact, once you get the hang of it, this device can become as natural as breathing. You may, of course, alter the line to make it comfortable for you. Some people prefer "What the. . . ?" (as in "What the heck is she doing here!") to the above "Oh!" Use whatever comes most easily to you.

Another version of this technique is the Mating Call. In this form of the Search, you make it obvious to the person or people you're itching to ditch that your mate is—or has been—signaling you to join him or her. If the subject from whom you are departing knows who your spouse is, you can execute the Mating Call without using words; you can merely roll your eyes in the direction of your mate as if to say, "He's calling me again!" Or nod or wave in the direction of your mate, appearing to answer his or her call. If, on the other hand, the subject is *not* familiar with your mate, you can say, "Oh . . . pardon me, my wife wants me . . . excuse me for a moment, will you?" The "for a moment" is a nice touch and can soften the exit. It implies you really would like to come back to continue the conversation, but it isn't a promise.

The Counterfeit Search is indubitably a bold maneuver, which is the very reason it works so well. People don't suspect this kind of lie; whereas, every time anyone excuses himself or herself for a drink or something to eat, it smacks of escape. The other plus to this technique is its quality of positive energy: you will appear to have so many people you need to talk to that you can't remain in one place—you're just dashing madly here and there! It can lend you an air of popularity (except of course, if you use the Mating Call. Then you just look loyal, at best, or henpecked, at worst.)

EMERGENCY ESCAPE HATCHES

If you really want to improve your mingling skills, I strongly suggest you learn and practice at least some of the nine escape maneuvers. For extreme circumstances, however, or if you are the kind of person who freezes when you feel cornered at a party, you can memorize one or more of the following emergency escape lines. They can be a little brutal, but they're quick and easy.

Note: You may have the most success with these if your delivery is accompanied by a slight touch of your hand on the other person's arm. It's always a good idea to be as warm as possible when you're leaving someone high and dry.

"Hold that thought . . ."

"I'll be right back . . ."

"Excuse me, it's too loud (smoky, hot) in here . . ."

"I'm sorry—I just remembered something."

"Got to go mingle!"

"Excuse me just a minute . . ."

"I'm not feeling well . . ."

"Excuse me, . . . it's my contact lens . . ."

"I think I just lost a filling . . ."

"Oh my GOD—my wallet!"

YOUR EXIT OF LAST RESORT: THE OFFENSIVE ESCAPE

Unlike the nine exit maneuvers and the Emergency Escape Hatches, which are more or less *defensive* in nature, the following *offensive* ploys are last-resort, fight-fire-with-fire techniques. They are to be used *only* when faced with the most torturous bores, bigots, and bad guys. Instead of *your* leaving, you make the other person leave *you*.

After my brother told me about this passive-aggressive exit strategy, I began asking others about it. Not too many people would admit to ever using this method; however, most of the *men* I interviewed related without hesitation to the idea. In fact, it seemed quite familiar to them, while women seemed horrified at the notion.

Before I describe the various ways to effect the Offensive Escape, I must warn you: What you're about to do might make people dislike you, or at least think you are very strange. Usually the Offensive Escape necessitates your becoming so undesirable yourself, that the person or people you want to escape will actually be desperate to get away from *you*! Do not use this method unless you have a strong ego and unless it's impossible that you will ever again need the good opinion of the people you are about to "offend." Also, know that if your technique works, you are going to be left alone (though one assumes that anyone courageous enough to undertake this will be able to handle that). And the very worst-case possibility: The offensive thing you've said or done will get around at the party. In other words, you run the risk of becoming a Party Leper.

Still, there's something exhilarating, something daring and wild, about the following Offensive Escape tactics. So, if you're really stuck, or you are truly incensed by someone:

- **Make the person interested in talking to someone else.** This is the least offensive Offensive Escape, and I have used it with great success. Point out someone else in the room and tell the person from whom you would like to escape, "Oh look, there she is! . . . That woman over there confessed to me secretly that she was dying to meet you." Or "I'm sworn to secrecy, but there's someone in that group there who is giving out hundred dollar bills." Or wave in the general direction of a group and say "I think you're being summoned." When your victim looks confused and asks who, tell him, "I can't see him now, but he was waving to you . . . over there." There are countless ways of seducing the person to leave you (you can tell him the food is disappearing fast or there's only one bottle of champagne left), and the great thing is, you can keep inventing until something works!

- **Speak very loudly and quickly.** This is a way of becoming, presumably, more obnoxious than the obnoxious person you are trying to flee from. Note: This is bound to attract some attention, and some people will think you are pretty nutty. But it *will* work.

- **Act like you have a disease.** I can't recommend this, but I've heard it can be effective. Ask the person if she sees a rash anywhere on your face. When she says no, nod uncertainly and say, "Oh. Good . . . thanks."

- **Talk about personal hygiene.** I'm afraid I can't give you any examples; my grandmother would turn over in her grave. (You have to be *extremely* desperate to try this one.)

- **Be stupid and/or boring.** Describe what you saw sold on the Shopping Channel. Use lots of "ums" as you talk, and speak as slowly as possible without letting the other person interrupt.

- **Make the person self-conscious.** Tell her she's got food on her face, or that her slip is showing. Better yet, be cryptic about what's wrong; say something like, "I don't have any mirrors at home either."

- **Become a Fanatic.** As intensely as you can, ask, "Do you have a personal relationship with Jesus Christ?"

- **Spill something on the person.** Food, your drink, their drink, anything. This is fast and effective; they'll not only be disenchanted with you but also will need to go in search of water and a towel.

- **Step on the person's foot or otherwise hurt him.** Be careful with this. Remember, we live in a litigious society. You don't really want to hurt the other person. You also don't want to get hit, or cause a scene. Causing a scene of any kind is not conducive to mastering the art of mingling.

·5·

FANCY FOOTWORK: ADVANCED MINGLING TECHNIQUES

O nce you have some basic maneuvers down, you may want to try to expand your mingling repertoire and begin to "fine tune" your mingling style. Remember: The more versatile and practiced you become as a mingler, the more enjoyment you will get from your social encounters, and the easier it will be to achieve whatever secondary goals you might have (getting a job, getting a promotion, getting a date). And, though most readers may not immediately be able to conquer every one of the following techniques and tricks, I think you'll find many of them familiar, and some of them invaluable!

FIVE MINGLING STYLES FOR THE WELL-SCHOOLED

• The Quick-Change Artist •

The more you come to understand the art of mingling, the more you will see the importance of being in control of your conversations. A true mingling artist virtually molds each encounter using various tools of his trade; the most powerful one being the ability to change subjects easily. Most "natural-born" minglers have this Quick-Change talent without even realizing it, and unless they are mingling purely by entertaining, the Quick Change is probably their forte—the thing that makes them indestructible mingling machines.

To become a proficient Quick-Change Artist, you need to practice shifting your focus a bit during conversation, so that as you listen to the other person speak, you concentrate not only on your response to the person's comment or question, but also on where you want the conversation to go next. I don't mean that you should not pay attention to the present conversation. The best minglers always appear to be fascinated by whatever is being said to them. But if you are on your toes, you can be ready to effect a swift transition to a subject of *your* choosing before the people around you even know what hit them.

A good way to think about the process involved in the Quick Change is to imagine building a bridge. You and your conversational partners are currently on one side of the river; you want the group to be on the other side. The key is to find some material with which to build a bridge from one side to the other. If you just interrupt and change the subject without making a connection between the old topic and the new one, you will usually come off sounding awkward, even rude. Remember: It can't look as if you have consciously manipulated the direction of the conversation; the dialogue must appear to flow naturally, as if it is taking its own course.

Let's say your conversational group is composed of a very interesting architect, the architect's husband, and another person. You would like to steer the conversation around to the architect, as you have seen her buildings and admired them. At present, however, the architect's husband is going on at length about his garden, which you find about as interesting as cardboard. Everyone else is standing there, passively listening, or throwing in comments such as "Oh I've seen those, they're beautiful." or "Do those bloom all year round?" As a Quick-Change Artist, you can decide exactly where you want to be, conversationally, and it should take you no time at all to get there. Just conjure up all the possible connections between the two subjects, select one, and then head for the bridge.

For instance, you can turn to the architect and say something like, "Planning houses in a community is like planting a garden in a way, isn't it?" or "Do you work closely with the landscapers on the gardens and lawns for your buildings?" The architect will answer, and you will be able to continue in your chosen course of conversation, taking pride in the fact that you have succeeded in creating a more interesting environment not only for yourself, but also (probably) for at least two of the other three people in your clique.

Admittedly, some subjects are harder to get away from than others. And there are some people who are adamantly determined to talk about whatever it is they are determined to talk about. But if you really get good at changing subjects, you can outmaneuver anyone, and/or escape if necessary.

Another way to approach the Quick Change is to use free association. This method can really keep the ball in your court, which is where you want it, because it's always an advantage if *you* get to serve. For example, if someone is chattering away about flowers, take the word "flower" and let it lead you to another word, the first word that pops into your mind. In other words, think "flower—bee." Then you can ask, as if it is really puzzling you, whether or not bees pollinate *all* flowers, or just some. When the floral expert answers, you can then safely complete the subject switch by remarking that you have an uncommon fear of bees, or that you are allergic to bees, or did everyone know that after bees sting you they die, and isn't that true justice? This last remark can lead to a discussion of aggression and justice, which can end up being a whole lot more interesting than flowers and fertilizer.

Free association is used often by the Quick-Change Artist, for two reasons. First, it's more flexible and open-ended than bridge-building. That is, you aren't necessarily trying to get from point A to point B; you are simply moving away from point A, either because A is boring or distasteful to you or because you want to be in control of the dialogue. The other reason free association works so well for the Quick-Change Artist is that the subject you move to is probably right on the tip of everyone else's brain, also. The change will usually seem perfectly natural and not at all forced. A good Quick-Change Artist can, in this manner, lead the conversation of a whole group rapidly and elegantly from one topic to another, so that everyone—including the Artist himself—has a good time.

• The Playful Plagiarist •

Have you ever been in a wedding reception line where you had to talk to hundreds of people, one right after the next? You probably had absolutely no idea what to say to any of them, and your face started to hurt from trying to smile so much. It was while in such a desperate situation that I—happily—stumbled upon the Playful Plagiarist style of mingling. It's perfect for reception lines, award ceremonies, and other occasions where you are the center of attention (your coming-out party, your art opening) and people are coming at you, fast and furious.

Let's say you are the maid of honor at a wedding. As if it weren't bad enough that you have to stand there in a horrible pink polyester chiffon maid-of-honor getup, you are being forced to stand in your dyed-to-match, uncomfortable pumps and shake hands with an unending stream of guests, most of whom you don't know and couldn't care less if you ever saw again. You have only a couple of minutes to speak with each person, and because all you *really* want is for reception-line duty to be over so you can have a drink or something to eat, your natural tendency is to take a totally passive stance; that is, to smile as nicely as possible and say "thank you" to the obligatory comment that you certainly do look beautiful.

This is, of course, perfectly acceptable social behavior. But if you consider the fact that the guests moving through the line are just as bored as you are at having to take part in this outmoded reception-line ritual, why not try to make it fun? Having fun is, after all, your objective in every mingling situation. And believe me, if you can make interesting conversation in a wedding reception line, the word is going to get around that you are a social success. Here's what you do.

Take something someone says to you, and use it on the next person who approaches you, as if it is your own idea. For example, if Mrs. Smithers says to you in parting how nice it is that the bride and groom found each other after all these years, when Mr. Johnson greets you next, you can ask him if *he* doesn't think it's wonderful that the bride and groom have found each other. Then when Mr. Johnson says, yes, they make a lovely couple, you can say to the next person, don't Joe and Sally make a lovely couple? And when that person says Oh yes, she's never seen such a beautiful bride, the next thing on your lips can be a remark about how the bride is the loveliest bride *you've* ever seen.

By using the Playful Plagiarist, you can avoid using one line over and over and at the same time, you don't have to think up new things to say at sixty miles per hour. Even though the examples I have given are things it might not be too hard to think up yourself, in tiring mingling situations it's much more relaxing if you let others do some of the work. A little conversational petty theft, and people will get the impression you have a natural social sense. In fact, it will appear as if you are never at a loss for words.

The Playful Plagiarist technique can be useful in "normal" party circumstances also, though it may call for a little more panache in its execution. At a typical large party, using this style requires taking a line or comment you hear in one group with you and delivering it when you are safely inside another group (sometimes you can even use it as an entrance line). For example, if someone remarks that this is the tenth party your host has had in one year, the next time you are in another group of people and in need of something to say, you can repeat the line, especially as it is a general party observation and will fit in at just about any pause.

Warning: Occasionally, someone may *recognize* your stolen line as having come from someone other than you, either because there's a witness from the first group present or because the comment has unmistakable characteristics. If you think there's any possibility of getting caught with your hand in the till, the best thing to do is give authorship: Start or follow the line with "So-and-so told me . . ." That way no one will think of you as an unoriginal sap who is reduced to stealing bits of conversation—yet you still get to use the material!

• Trivial Pursuits •

Some people have a gift for remembering bits of trivia; others (like me) don't. There's no way that I know of to change a non-trivia-minded person into one of those human fact magnets we all know and love. However, if you *are* an automatic storer of trivia, you have a great asset to your mingling style, as long as you keep in mind the following:

1. **If you've got it, flaunt it.** If you do have interesting tidbits of information at your fingertips, by all means share them. Trivia and mingling are close cousins—they're both light, interesting, nonthreatening human interaction. But keep it within reason, please. No one enjoys talking to someone who spews trivia every time he opens his mouth.

2. **Wait for an appropriate place in the discussion.** This is absolutely essential in playing the mingling game of Trivial Pursuits. Your fun fact must be relevant to the conversation and be offered up at just the right place, so it doesn't seem forced, or as if you are showing off your trivia prowess.

3. **Don't maneuver the conversation for the sole purpose of delivering a piece of trivia.** This is taboo, even though good minglers have the skill to do it. If the item you have is so earth-shatteringly fascinating that you feel compelled to repeat it, just jump in and do it, if you must. But don't spend time and energy manipulating the discussion so that your piece of trivia will fit in. You may get caught at it, and that can be *very* embarrassing. In fact, to put it bluntly, you could end up looking like a Trivia Nerd. Trivia buffs are considered entertaining only if they are not too obsessed with their trivia.

4. **Make sure of your audience.** Watch carefully when you deliver your first trivial fact. Do the others in the group seem interested? Sometimes people find certain trivia to be an intrusion in the flow of dialogue, or even boring. There's no way to tell whether or not you use trivia well except to study the reactions of those around you. Do eyes roll or glance away? Do you hear a lot of throat clearing? Make sure you're not being obnoxious.

• The Art of Piggybacking •

Piggybacking is a very familiar concept in mingling, and I know many people who swear by it as a mingling style. It's not exactly the most *courageous* tack to take, but it can be used continually, from your first opening line up until the time you leave the party.

Many minglers use this technique without thinking about it, it's so simple. It entails merely attaching yourself briefly to another person to get from one place to another.

Imagine that you arrive at a party where just about the only person you know is the hostess. No problem. Just latch on to that hostess and hang on for dear life (figuratively speaking), until such time as she leads you over to someone else and introduces you—or until someone new joins you and the hostess. Have no fear, for one of these two things will happen within minutes, if she's any kind of hostess at all. Now you have a new acquaintance to tag along with, and you can follow this person into another group, where you can find new people to trail. In this way you can leapfrog from conversation to conversation, always appearing to have many friends and never at a loss for a conversational companion. Even if, for some reason, the hostess *doesn't* hook you up with another guest but just gestures to the far end of the room and says, "Feel free to help yourself at the bar," you can still employ the Piggyback technique—after you've introduced yourself to one or two people using other methods first.

The real art of Piggybacking lies in the *way* you follow people. You are *not* encouraged to actually hold on to coattails or skirts during this maneuver. Like a good gumshoe tailing someone, pretend you don't notice when your Piggybacking target leaves the circle of people; wait a few seconds, and then casually follow in his wake. Remember the Changing of the Guard escape technique? It's very easy to move right after someone else has exited, if you do it quickly enough. The idea is to make your target think, when he sees you've followed him into a new group, that it's only a coincidence, or that you found his conversation interesting enough to want more of it. Never let him know that you are using him to help you move in and out of groups; get caught doing the Piggyback, and people will think you are a real baby.

Please note: It's essential that you remember to switch piggyback targets as often as possible. It's against the basic rules of mingling to stay with one person for any substantial length of time. Never forget my earlier maxim: *He who mingles best, mingles alone.* (Of course, I never said you couldn't occasionally have a little help.)

• The Butterfly Flit •
(EXPERTS ONLY)

Picture a country meadow on a summer day. In fact, if you can, go *visit* a country meadow on a summer day. Watch how the butterfly dances lightly upon the flowers. Notice how quickly and gently she touches each one—barely brushing like a whisper over some while resting gracefully for long moments on others. The butterfly flies free; each flower she visits is honored by her brief stay, and each perfumed encounter becomes forever a part of her fluttering experience.

Pardon me for waxing poetic, but this is the image you must hold in your mind while attempting the challenging Butterfly Flit. It is with this technique that mingling becomes an art form, and like any true art, it is hard to describe in concrete terms or by using step-by-step directions.

The Butterfly Flit can encompass any or all of the techniques, lines, and tricks in this book. Using all the mingling knowledge and instinct at your disposal, your objective is to weave your way through the clusters of people, stopping for thirty seconds or so at each to check them out. If you decide a group is interesting or challenging enough for you to make a mingling commitment, you enter the group more fully, and remain for a five- or six-minute period. Then you're off again, leaving your ex-group breathless, wishing you had stayed longer and hoping you'll return soon.

Just exactly how, choreographically, you manage the Butterfly Flit without looking inane, or without being rude to anyone or knocking anything over, is too complicated to describe. If you are ever feeling truly inspired or socially brilliant, go ahead and give the Flit a whirl. It's one of those things you can learn only by doing. But, frankly, I do not recommend it for most minglers.

Six Gimmicks for the Confident Mingler

When the circumstances are right and you are feeling game, the following gimmicks can add spice to your evening and variety to your mingling experience. Unlike the mingling styles described above, however, mingling gimmicks are for *occasional* use only. Your limit per party should be one or two times for each trick.

• A Case of Mistaken Identity •

I know you've probably seen countless versions of this ploy in bad "B" movies. It's historically been used as a pick-up line, which is why I try never to use it except when I have no other motive (that I know of) but a purely conversational one. You guessed it; it's the old "Pardon me! I thought you were someone else!" This is such a cliché that it actually works, probably because most people can't believe that anyone would try this line if it weren't true.

There are many enjoyable and effective ways to carry off this daring opening maneuver. The easiest and safest is to come up behind your "mark" and confidently touch or tap them on the shoulder. Your big "I'm so glad to see you" smile should fade by the time the person finishes turning around, and be replaced by a confused, sheepish, surprised look. Then you can say something like, "I'm so sorry . . . from the back, I swear, you look just like someone else." I sometimes even like to add, "God that sounds like a line, doesn't it?" In any case, by this time you've more or less entered the group and you can go ahead and follow your Mistaken Identity entrée with any number of conversational moves, including just plain introducing yourself.

There are, as you can imagine, more outrageous ways to use A Case of Mistaken Identity, all of which can make a lasting impression but can also get you into trouble. You can pinch the person, pour a drink over his head, slap him smartly on the back (or elsewhere), even kiss him on the neck. All of these things imply an intimacy that *must* be equalled by your embarrassment when you discover your "mistake." The drawback with these more extreme versions: Often the victim is so offended and the other people in the group so startled, that the thought of actually joining them becomes distasteful to you.

Always remember, however, that should this gimmick backfire and you find yourself greeted with hostility or any other non-welcoming behavior, the very nature of the lie will allow you to withdraw without losing face. After all, it wasn't the person you were looking for, right? You didn't mean to approach this group anyway; it was all a mistake. With a parting apology, you're out of it, free and clear, ready to try it again (on someone on the other side of the room, please) or to put away the gimmick for another day.

• Fumbling In •

A lot of these techniques may seem a bit crude, but advanced mingling doesn't mean subtle or quiet; it only means that the methods require more skill or finesse. So while Fumbling In may seem like a rough-and-tumble way of entering a conversation, it actually takes an accomplished mingler to perform it correctly.

The perfect model for this gimmick is Peter Falk. His Columbo character, who seems on the surface to be a bumbling idiot, is really a brilliant tactician who can fool people with his clumsy act. It is with Columbo's particular form of graceless artfulness that you are going to approach this opening gambit.

Ready? Set? Go.

Select your target group. Edge toward them, making certain no member of the group is looking at you. With your back or at least your side to them, pretend to be concentrating hard on something across the room, and then . . . "accidentally" bump into someone in the group. Not too hard; for this particular trick, you don't want to cause spillage or injury. Just jostle them enough for at least one person to notice and acknowledge your presence. After you say you're terribly sorry, usually it is easy to join their conversation. If, on the other hand, you should be confronted with any hostility, like "Hey! Why'nt ja look where you're goin'!" have some believable explanation ready. "Someone pushed me," is always good, though I also like the more self-denegrating "I *am* sorry, really,

I don't know what is the matter with me—been a clumsy oaf all day!" With the latter excuse you still have a chance that your fumble will succeed; your taking responsibility for your klutziness may endear you to some of the group and overcome their initial bad humor.

The real beauty of Fumbling In is that, if the gimmick does fail and you are ignored or rebuffed, or if you decide that you made a bad selection and you don't want to stay in the group after all, it's the easiest thing in the world for you to move on. You can't be rejected, because you didn't *ask* to join their group; it was an accident! In effect, nothing has been ventured, and therefore nothing is lost.

Note: Fumbling In should be attempted only in a fairly crowded room. If there are miles of space between people, you're just going to look foolish; or worse, drunk. It's bad enough if you do get drunk at a party, but it's an absolute crime to *appear* drunk.

• The Interruption Eruption •
(EXPERTS ONLY)

Please pay attention to the "Experts Only" label on this one. Even I rarely attempt this stunt, though it's a heck of a lot of fun when it succeeds. You have to be feeling absolutely fearless.

But let's assume you *are* an expert mingler, with years of experience under your belt. You are at a fun party and are feeling adventuresome. You have just ducked smoothly out of a conversation you had grown weary of and are scanning the room for a new set of mingling partners. Suddenly, you spot it: a laughing, glittering cluster of four or five people over by the punch bowl. They look like a tight group, an invigorating challenge for you to try to enter. You quickly run through the many entrance maneuvers in your mind and decide on . . . the Interruption Eruption.

When you feel quite ready, you take a deep breath, move boldly up to the group, push your way firmly in between two people and say, loudly and with great energy, "Hello there! How are you all? Hey, I don't think I've met a single one of you yet! My name is . . ."

It's not so much what you say in the Interruption Eruption as how you say it. Your demeanor must communicate that you are so certain of your charms that you know that everyone will be happy that you've come to talk to them, even though you have more or less exploded, uninvited, into their conversation. As you may suspect, there is a dangerously thin line between this technique and being rude; so the important thing is to exude extreme warmth to everyone in the group after you are in. You must positively *beam* good will at everyone, and at the same time, you must lead the conversation for a while. People will expect you to perform after such an entrance.

You can use almost any line for the Interruption Eruption; you can even use a question, such as one of the Game-Playing questions on page 40 ("Excuse me! What color would you say this is?"). A question is usually a bit more abrasive here, but if it is a very good question, one that someone snaps up right away, it can be a quicker way in. The best kind of question to use is one that indicates an on going debate or poll-taking; such as, "When did *you* hear about the Smith company warehouse burning down?" Not only will your eagerness for information help excuse your interruption but also people tend to forget that you've barged in on them when there's an interesting query before them.

The Interruption Eruption is a strong, daring mingling gimmick, which can be positively thrilling when you are victorious. But if it doesn't work, you are in serious, serious trouble. One time I interrupted a group with a brazen, "Hi, guys! Gosh, isn't it hot in here?" Well, you might have thought I'd just shot someone. Everyone looked at me with a mixture of distaste and shock, and one man said, "Excuse me, Miss . . . whoever you are . . . we were in the middle of a conversation!" Upon which I slunk guiltily away, tail between my legs. But of course I recovered. And so will you.

• Movie Lines •

This is not about how to mingle while waiting in line for the movies, though that's not an uninteresting topic (see Lines on Line, page 140). No, Movie Lines refers to a very useful mingling device that can get you out of many diffculties. For some sticky situations—and especially in certain circles—this particular gimmick can be the ticket to total mingling success. If you have any sense of the dramatic at all, you will discover that if you aren't using this one already, you should be.

When someone says something to you that makes you feel uncomfortable, or if you find you are at a loss for something to say, you just pop in one of the following famous quotes from movies. Your listeners will love it. What you are actually doing is relieving psychological tension by calling forth a common cultural image. It almost always lightens the atmosphere, and it has the added benefit of being the kind of conversational punctuation mark that allows you to change the subject or even exit from the group. Two rules: the line must be very familiar to people, and you must quote it word for word (or almost).

Here are some of my favorites:

LINE

USE

"I think this is the beginning of a beautiful friendship." (Casablanca)

When flattered, or just for general comraderie

"Frankly, my dear, I don't give a damn!" (Gone with the Wind)

When insulted, or when dealing with a vicious gossip

"Years from now, when you talk of this—and you will—be kind." (Tea and Sympathy)

After a faux pas or social blunder

"Fasten your seatbelts. It's going to be a bumpy night." (All About Eve)

After having witnessed a scene of some kind

"That's a horse of a different color." (The Wizard of Oz)	When stalling for time, after having been asked something you don't know or would rather not answer
"It is a far, far better thing I do than I have ever done." (A Tale of Two Cities)	When leaving a group, after having been called away by someone, or asked to do something

• Using Accents •

If you want to add a little flair to your verbal exchanges, you might try Using Accents. It's a good thing to do when you feel the need to express yourself in an indirect way, when you are feeling uncomfortable, or when someone is really bugging you. **Caution**: the following contains cultural stereotypes that may be hazardous to your social health.

1. **The French accent.** Use "zee fronshe acsonte" when someone has just done something, said something, or served something that is overly fancy or expensive. For example, "Oh, look at zat! Zee hot dogs ere behing sayrved on zee crystalle platteres!" A helpful hint: When doing a French accent, raise your eyebrows as high as possible and frown. It will help your pronunciation; for some reason, most French people do this when they talk.

2. **The British accent.** An English accent can be a good way to let someone know you think they are acting snobby: "Oh rahley, dahling, I hed ebsolutely no ideah you would feel thet way!" Or if someone unpleasant has just left your group: "Rahther insinsitive chap, what?" It also comes in handy for certain faux pas—when you find you have not behaved in as formal or "correct" a manner as was appropriate. In these situations, using an accent helps you get over any embarrassment you might have, and a gentle poke at yourself shows those around you that you realize your

behavior wasn't quite "up to snuff." Usually a clipped "Sew sorry, ducky." will suffice.

3. **The Southern accent.** My personal favorite. I perfected this accent when I was in school in Virginia, and I have used it with great enjoyment for many years. For women, it's useful when someone makes an overtly sexist remark that you are not about to let pass unnoticed but that you want to be gracious about. For instance: "Well, fiddle-dee-dee! Mah poor little ol' head's just about to bust right open trying to figure all that out!" Also, if someone flatters you excessively, you can cover any embarrassment with a bit of Southern drawl: "I sway-ar, y'all is makin' me blush so, I just look like a little ol' tomatah!"

4. **The country bumpkin accent.** If you're not sure what a country bumpkin accent is, just think of TV's Gomer Pyle. Use this accent only when recovering from one of your own faux pas ("Ayuh, uh, I guess I missed ma mouth, ayup"), but never to make fun of someone else's. It's too mean.

There are lots of other accents, of course (Italian, German, Swedish, Indian, Valley Girl), any of which can be used to enhance your dialogue, depending on your own skill, inclination, imagination, and situation. You have to use accents sparingly, of course. For the most part, your "impersonation" should last no longer than a sentence or two, unless you are in a one-on-one mingle where the other person slips happily into the pretense with you. In that case, you can stay in the role a lot longer. But don't go whole-hog; nobody likes a ham.

Warning: Before using any accent, be absolutely certain that no one in your clique has a real one! In this case imitation will not be seen as flattery.

• Making the Most of Toasts •

Most people make toasts only at weddings or awards dinners. Toast-making at a sit-down dinner is a pretty straightforward proposition; but contrary to what you may think, a toast can be made anywhere, anytime—even while mingling.

"Anytime" is actually a slight exaggeration. You do have to have a glass in your hand to make a toast. But given that small requirement, you can throw one in at practically any place in the conversation, to accomplish various objectives. For instance, you can recover from a faux pas ("A toast! To carpet cleaners!"), soothe an argument ("Here's to a difference of opinion"), field an insult ("To charm! Why don't you go and get yourself some"), or even exit from a group ("To [whatever is being discussed] everywhere! Excuse me.").

You can throw in a toast in the more obvious situations, of course, such as after someone has just brought you a drink ("Here's looking at you—Thanks.") or after somebody makes an announcement ("To ———; the best of luck!"). You can also use toasts to change the subject, specifically to take the heat off yourself, if someone is asking you questions you'd rather not answer or making you uncomfortable with too much attention. Simply pick out someone else in your group and make a toast to him, or take the too-personal subject and make a toast to the subject in general.

Usually you will want to wait for a pause before proposing your toast. But often, if you simply raise your glass while someone is still talking, the person will stop—sometimes in mid-sentence—and you can make your toast. All of us are trained to stop whatever it is we are doing and pay close attention when someone raises a glass. Never forget that toasts are very powerful social weapons and that they can become an important part of your conversational arsenal.

Two toast tips: 1) Never down the entire contents of your glass after a toast, unless you have only a small amount left, or unless you are in a place (Russia, for example) where this is considered the norm. 2) If your glass is empty when someone proposes a toast, just raise the empty glass in tribute. *Don't* pretend to drink, and *don't* say, "Hold that toast until I get something in my glass."

SOPHISTICATED BODY BUSINESS

Not all mingling is done with the mouth. Your whole body speaks every time you move. Body language is important to learn for all areas of life, but for the would-be mingling expert, there are three particular pieces of body "business" you may want to study.

• The Mysterious Mingle •

The Mysterious Mingle is really about poise. So far in this book I have been talking about what you can say, when you should say it, and how you should say it. But there are times in mingling when the best line to use is no line at all.

To carry off this technique, you must project the attitude that you have a great many fascinating things to say, but that *tonight* you'd rather listen to others and kind of soak up life. Some Mysterious Minglers prefer to put a little "ho-hum" feeling into their presentation; others lean more toward the intriguing "I've got a secret" look. In either case, your posture must be erect but nonchalant, and your facial expression should be attentive, pleasant, and, above all, confident. It may help you to employ the Lucky Star survival fantasy (page 5), at least for the first time you try this.

As you move through the room, keep your arms and legs relaxed, and don't hurry anywhere. The world is your oyster. Life is a bowl of cherries. You are going to listen contentedly to conversation, and answer thoughtfully when called upon, but never with more than a few words. Use an enigmatic smile whenever you can (practice this beforehand in the mirror; it has to *look* enigmatic, not just feel it). Whether you are quietly entering a group (this is the only time you're allowed to use the Fade-in without completing the maneuver by saying something), exiting a group, or just standing by yourself somewhere, remember: You are not at a loss for words, you've just put them away for now. By choice. Your body stance, your eyes, mouth, eyebrows—every part of you—has got to say, "I like people very much but I really don't care at all what they think of me."

There's something very powerful about a person who does not talk when everyone else is working so hard at conversation. If you do the Mysterious Mingle well, people will be so interested in trying to find out what your story is and why you're not talking about it, that you could find yourself becoming—silently—the center of attention.

Two words of warning: It's not a good idea to try to get away with a Mysterious Mingle pose when you suddenly find you can't think of anything to say. People will sense the difference, unless you are an extremely good actor. And there are, after all, other, much easier things to do when you draw a blank. Also, be sure you are coming off as *mysterious* and not *supercilious*. You don't want people to think you're stuck up.

• The Touchy-Feely Mingle •

Never underestimate the power of human touch. A small amount of the right kind of touching while you are mingling can add a comforting sense of warm intimacy to your conversations. The wrong kind of touching, however, or too much touching, can be one of the most serious faux pas you can make without taking off all your clothes.

In following the directions for the Touchy-Feely Mingle, always err on the side of not enough rather than too much. If you have to, tell yourself you have only so many touches to give out for the whole night so you have to use them sparingly. And please: Don't even try it if you've had a lot to drink.

Use the Touchy-Feely only when you are involved in a fairly absorbing conversation with one other person. It doesn't exactly have to be a tête-à-tête—there can be others standing with you in the group—but you and this other person should be doing most of the talking. Watch the other person's face carefully to see if he or she is truly engaged in the discussion. At an appropriate place during a time when you are speaking (the punch line of a joke, the climax of a story, the main point in a discussion) lean forward slightly and clasp or touch the person's forearm or upper arm briefly, then let go. It should be not *quite* a squeeze, yet more than just a brush. Now—and this is important—regard the person carefully during this touch, watching in particular the eyes. You should be able to tell if your touch has enhanced the exchange or hindered it. Unless you are certain that the effect was a positive one, *do not* touch this person again.

Other types of Touchy-Feely mingling: resting your hand briefly on the shoulder of someone standing next to you; touching someone lightly on the back (not the small of the back, please, that's a little *too* intimate for mingling); taking someone's elbow as you move across the room together. For the most part, any other kind of touching during mingling is unacceptable.

The Touchy-Feely Mingle, when done with sensitivity, can make a five-minute conversation a warmer, more enjoyable experience. But remember, a little goes a long way. There's nothing quite so unpleasant as being repeatedly pawed by some thick-skulled lout.

• The Beauty of Bowing •

The beauty of bowing is threefold: hardly anyone does it anymore; it can communicate many different things; and it's classy. Bowing is an excellent nonverbal device—elegant, humorous, and effective—for both men *and* women (the curtsy, thank God, went out with smelling salts). I recommend trying at least one of the following bows, just to see how it feels.

THE BOW	MEANING
A friendly, small bow, leaning forward slightly from the waist,	Greetings. I'm happy to have you join us.

retaining eye contact and accompanied by a sincere smile.

A medium to small bow of either just the head or the whole upper body, eyes close during bow; smile optional.	Yes (or I agree).
A very slight inclination of the head and neck, along with a slow closing of the eyes and just the hint of a wry smile.	Touché.
A fairly deep bow of the head, done with one or two hands on the chest and a grateful but closed-mouth smile.	Thank you kindly for the compliment, Sir or Madam (tongue-in-cheek).
A full, dramatic bow from the waist, one hand on the stomach and the other hand on the back. The head turns slightly to the side. Stay in bowed position for one or two seconds before coming back to an upright position.	My story is over. Thank you for listening.
With hands clasped in front of you as if in prayer, a bow of the head, neck, and shoulders. Close eyes briefly while bowing.	I defer to your greater wisdom in the matter.
Deep, full-bodied bow, arms dramatically outstretched; eyes open or closed; turn away as you come back up.	Good-bye, it's been an honor to talk to you.

| Click your heels together sharply; stand up stiffly at attention, then bow fully and quickly in mock military fashion. No smile. | You're such a fascist; I'm not even going to honor that remark with a response. |

CONVERSATION PIECES: USING PROPS AND ACCESSORIES

• Jewelry, Hats, and Other Attire •

I don't think there is any single trick in mingling that works so well, so easily, and so often as having your own mingling prop of some kind. While purists might cast a scornful eye on the use of these obvious and common mingling crutches, I believe that anything that helps you have a good time at a party is legit. In fact, I used to wear an attention-getting accessory to almost every social function I attended.

Whether it's a feather hat or a pin that says "I like Ike," wearing an unusual accessory almost guarantees that you'll never have to endure the trauma of the Awkward Silence. Invariably, the first (or second) thing people will say to you is "Wow, what a wonderful (odd, awful, unique, colorful)————that is!" Not only does this prop provide them with easy subject matter—for which any minglephobic is always grateful—but it also causes them to introduce a topic for which you're totally prepared. You are now on home turf, since it's *your* accessory, after all, and you have probably already had many conversations about it. You have stored up a wealth of material from which to choose (where you got the particular pin, about wearing pins in general, the origin of pin wearing, etc.), and you've already rehearsed your lines.

The best conversation pieces by far are hats and earrings. (When men started wearing earrings I thought, "Great, they've finally caught on to the tools of the art of mingling!") Hats and earrings work best because they are worn on the head. Once you get below the head—with ties, necklaces, pins and scarves—you are in more personal territory; things that are attached to the rest of the body—even the neck—enter the area of clothing. And most people will at least hesitate before commenting on your clothing.

A quick word about wearing unusual makeup. I have found from personal experience that weird or overdone makeup—huge beauty marks, false eyelashes, glitter blush—can be risky. It can alienate you from some people at a party while making you almost *too* interesting to what may be the more bizarre element. This is certainly okay, of course, as long as it is what you mean to do. I myself used to wear various odd "disguises" to fraternity parties in order to make a point. But when you do decide to go as far as wearing strange makeup, you should be aware that you are making more of a social statement than you do with a conversation piece. And be sure you know what it is you're saying.

Here is a list of accessories, in order of effectiveness, that can enhance your mingling experience. Pick an accessory that is particularly beautiful, funny, hip, unusual, thought-provoking—or handmade by you!

A hat or head piece

A briefcase or purse

Earring(s)

A ring

Sunglasses

A watch or bracelet

A tie

Gloves

A necklace

Stockings, socks

A pin

Shoes

A scarf

A fan★

★Fans would be too theatrical in some circles. But in the South, on a hot day, they're still considered au courant.

• Cigarettes as Props: Pros and Cons •

It's getting harder and harder for cigarette-smokers to smoke anywhere now, much less have the fun with their props that I used to. Almost as hard as giving up smoking for me was giving up the use of *the* coolest, most extraordinary, most beautiful cigarette case anyone has ever seen. It was made of sleek, blue-and-white Art Deco plastic and contained fourteen separate cylindrical compartments that held one cigarette each. It was elegantly designed and was held together with springs, so that when you bent it in two you would expose exactly one cigarette. Whenever I took out this case, people would ooh and aah and ask to examine it. It was a superb mingling prop. But I never knew just what a treasure I had until one fateful night in Chicago.

My friend Cathy and I had decided to check out a bar we had heard was "fun." We weren't familiar with the neighborhood, and when we got there, I knew why. The cab left us before we had a chance to turn back. Oh well, we said to each other, how bad could it be? We certainly weren't going to be chicken.

P.S. We should have been chicken. A big hairy guy with rings in his nose let us in. A smirk on his face plainly said, "These little girls don't know what they've just gotten themselves into." We looked around nervously. This was back in the early eighties, when punk bars were really punk—violent, scary places with chains and knives and danger—not the pseudo-punk clubs of today. Cathy and I didn't know much about punk bars then. But we were about to find out.

Everyone, literally everyone, stopped talking when we came in. (I might mention that we were wearing fifties-style swing skirts and sweaters with sweet little pearl buttons.) All we could see were big hairy tatoos with arms attached and dark, scabby faces, staring intensely at us.

Gulping, we stepped gingerly up to the bar and tried to act as though we were not in terrible trouble. The bartender, a huge man with a couple of safety pins through his cheek, leaned toward us and glared.

"Uh . . . um . . ." I managed to say, "A dry martini, please?" Cathy smiled a brave, gay smile. "And a Miller Lite?"

Silence. Nobody moved. Panic was closing in; I could feel Cathy tensing. Any minute we were going to have to just get up and run, but run where?

I decided I needed a cigarette. And that's when it happened. As soon as the bartender spotted my cigarette case, he growled, "Hey, lemme see that thing." Shaking, I handed it to him. He studied it, opened it, and then . . . he smiled.

In that split second, the entire bar relaxed. Our bartender, who turned out to be a rather decent fellow named Chris, showed the case to everyone in the place, and we were immediately accepted, 100 percent. The cigarette case had, miraculously, been our ticket in (and I even got it back). This mingling prop saved the day; in fact, we ended up having a surprisingly good time.

Now, I'm not saying that your cigarettes or cigarette props will keep you from being killed as mine did for me, but there is no question that cigarettes and cigarette paraphernalia (cases, lighters, and holders) can give you something to do as well as something to talk about. But let's look at the pros and cons of using cigarettes as props.

PROS

1. You can use cigarettes to ward off nervousness, as well as to affect the Lucky Star fantasy (see page 5) if you are using as your Lucky Star someone like Bette Davis.

2. You will bond immediately and totally with any other smokers at the party; in this day and age when smokers are such outcasts, they look upon each other practically as blood relatives, or at least fellow members of the secret underground.

3. You can use your cigarette "toys" as well as your particular brand of cigarette, as conversation pieces. You can also talk at great length about how and when you are going to quit.

4. You can use cigarette humor: You can get one of those telescope holders that expand to be a foot long; then when someone says to you "Nice cigarette holder," you can suddenly extend the thing to its full length and say "Thanks, I'm trying to stay away from cigarettes."

5. You can make people go away. Smoking can be a wonderful offensive technique. If someone is bothering you, just light up and blow smoke in his face.

CONS

1. You will be an annoyance to many, if not most, people at the party.

2. You may have to spend a lot of time looking for an ashtray.

3. While you are smoking, you limit your available pool of conversation partners. Many people do bolt at the sight or smell of cigarettes.

4. You may be paired with people you'd really like to avoid; if you're both smokers, it sort of binds you together (sharing an ashtray, matches, having to stand near a window).

5. You can get addicted. I don't mean addicted to tobacco, I mean addicted to using cigarettes as props. People do tend to get overly attached to their props.

Obviously, if you are a heavy smoker, you are more or less stuck with cigarettes as props. So if you must smoke, make the most of your habit and concentrate on the pros. But if you are a "social smoker," you may want to weigh the pros and cons carefully. It's a good idea to check out who the other smokers are—as they will become your roommates at the party—as well as how your host or hostess feels about smoking on the premises.

• The Hors D'Oeuvre Maneuver •

If you feel as if you need some kind of prop, but you've neglected to bring one with you, it may be the right time for the Hors D'Oeuvre Maneuver. This technique is somewhat aggressive, but it serves two purposes: it provides you with a piece of conversation, and it helps you move around the room freely.

You may be someone who has always had trouble circulating from one group to another and would like to try it with some mingling "training wheels." First, get permission from your host or hostess to pass a tray of food throughout the room. Try to select the yummiest items from the buffet table, and then just set off into the room. You won't have to worry about opening lines. Believe me, the minute people see you coming with those goodies, they will open a path for you. In fact, if the food you are carrying is good enough, you can just stay in one place and end up with a crowd around you.

The best thing about this mingling method? It's automatic.

Carrying a tray of food doesn't just *allow* you to mingle, it actually *forces* you to mingle, as it would be rude to the other guests to stay too long with one group of people.

Drawbacks: The Hors D'Oeuvre Maneuver is a pretty obvious mingler's aid; some people may consider you a coward. Also, you may find that the conversation, while you and your tray are present in the group, is limited to the food. In other words, people may associate you too much with the food. And most important to remember: If you are passing food, you can't be eating it at the same time. Eating off the tray you are passing is impolite. This can end up being too much torture to be worth it.

WORKING THE BAR OR FOOD AREA

When asked what is the first thing they do upon arriving at a party, almost everyone I know has the same answer: They go get something to eat or drink. I usually do the same thing myself. It's a perfectly natural thing to do. But make sure you recognize the bar or food area not just as a place to sate your hunger or thirst but as a vibrant mingling center, complete with props and pitfalls.

I myself fell into one of those pitfalls at a Christmas party. The food table was laden with various delicacies; and my undoing was some particularly exquisite smoked salmon placed at the head of the table. Smoked salmon is a passion of mine, and I'm ashamed to say I get quite greedy when I'm around it. I was doing a little mingling, but more or less hovering over the salmon, until I got an uneasy feeling I couldn't quite put my finger on. I mused over it as I took my tenth piece of salmon. Then it hit me. Instead of using the food area for mingling purposes, I had been using my mingling ability to get to the food! Specifically, to get to the salmon.

Never forget your primary goal is mingling. Food and drink should be a secondary part of your fun, and they can also serve as minglers' helpers in and of themselves. Just keep in mind a few simple rules as you are mingling in the food or bar area:

1. **Don't camp out by the bar or buffet.** Not only could you end up getting drunk or sick (or both), but also it isn't considerate to hog all the eats. (Also, some people won't have a chance to get near the bar or food if others won't move.) This rule is most important with respect to the bar. I know too many people who use their own minglephobia as an excuse to stand by the bar and guzzle drinks. Soon they find they have enough confidence to talk to anybody. But will anybody want to talk to them? If you want to get intoxicated, then by all means, get intoxicated. Just don't do it because you're afraid to mingle sober.

2. **Offer to help others get food or drink, to choose something, or slice them something.** If you are standing next to each other, it's an excellent mingling ploy to help another person in some small way, even holding their drink for them while they cut a piece of cheese. It endears you to the other person, shows you are a nice guy, and they more or less have to talk to you at least a little afterwards, lest they be discourteous.

3. **Talk about the food and the presentation.** Party food makes for great, safe conversation. Talk about any unusual foods, ask another person if she knows what's in that dip, or to recommend something. But don't overdo it. Let the subject of the food eventually lead you somewhere else, conversationally.

4. **Avoid making negative comments about any of the food unless the other person starts it.** You never know who is responsible for the cooking. Even if you are positive that no one at the party made any of the food, you could still inadvertently insult someone; the dish could be exactly

like one they make at home or brought to someone else's party last week.

5. **Try not to point with food or gesture with drinks.** It's unattractive and accidents can happen.

6. **Don't monopolize the bartender's time.** It's okay to talk to anyone, including the bartender, but do remember he's there to work. The host or hostess, as well as thirsty guests, may not appreciate your slowing him down.

7. **Make use of the time you are in a line for food or drink.** It's the one place where it doesn't look funny if you aren't talking to anyone. If you're lucky, you'll have someone to talk to while waiting, but if not, you can use the time to scope out the party and map out a mingling campaign.

Always remember: The food is there not just to eat,
but to aid you with the people you meet.

WHAT TO DO WHEN YOU'RE THE HOST

We all know people who are fabulous hosts or hostesses: people whose parties you never want to miss, and whose houses you never want to leave. What makes them such good hosts? Simple. They do more than open their doors and provide food and drink. They make certain that everyone has a good time.

The best hostess story I ever heard was about a dinner party during which one of the guests, who had had a little too much to drink, knocked over a full glass of red wine onto the table. The table was covered in a fine white linen tablecloth, and what made the incident even worse was that the employer of both the hostess and the tipsy guest was present. There was a moment of stunned silence and then, quick as a flash, the hostess made a sudden, sweeping motion with her hand, knocking over her own glass of wine. "Look how clumsy we all are tonight," she laughed, completely saving the day for the abashed, inebriated guest.

Not many hosts will go quite that far to put their guests at ease. But any self-respecting host should make sure that his guests are in fact mingling, and that no one is left standing morosely off by him- or herself. The host is, in effect, the mingling "coach" for the evening, and makes it his responsibility to see that people are mixing. Basically, what the host does throughout the entire night is similar to the Human Sacrifice escape technique, except that it is for more altruistic purposes. He talks to someone for a few minutes, then leads that person over to someone else. A good host doesn't then merely introduce the two people, he offers them something they have in common; in other words, he provides them with their first bit of subject matter, just to get things moving. Then he's off, to do the same thing again for two or three other people he has spotted who aren't talking to each other. Any "singles" of any kind—be they shy wallflowers or the obnoxious ones everyone else at the party is trying to get away from—must be "married" by the conscientious host—even drunks and bores (the host who's really on the ball will match these kinds up together).

Certainly it's okay for a host to have a little selfish mingle of his own now and then that has nothing to do with helping anybody else have a good time. But the host's personal conversation time per group should be shorter than the normal time, and he must make sure he spends a few moments—no matter how brief—with every single person who sets foot in his home. (Even if it's somebody's cousin who wasn't even invited.) It helps, of course, that a host has no need of exit lines; the mere fact of his hosthood will enable him to say "Excuse me," graciously at any time during any conversation. Everyone understands the duties of a host. However, the party-giver's real enjoyment should come from watching his own hostly handiwork: the knitting of his friends or colleagues together. (A helpful hint to the host: If space will allow it, place your bar area at one end of the room and your food at the other. That way people will be forced to move back and forth, and it will do a lot to promote mingling.)

It goes without saying that no host should ever drink too much at his own party. In addition to the many obvious reasons for this, being a host is a major responsibility, like being mother and father to the whole party. You definitely need all your faculties intact.

·6·

DRASTIC MEASURES: HANDLING UNUSUAL SITUATIONS

LIE OR DIE

L et's say you memorize fifty brilliant opening lines, and that you have all the right props; let's say you even master the Butterfly Flit. Now you're an expert in the art of mingling, right?

Not necessarily. The true test of whether you are a good mingler lies not in what you do under normal circumstances but in what you do in an emergency. Being able to handle yourself well in unexpected or unusual mingling situations takes concentration, imagination, flexibility, and—by far the most important ingredient: the unhesitating, unwavering ability to *lie through your teeth*.

I can't stress enough how important the white lie is in mingling, especially when you are faced with imminent disaster of some kind. It can be absolutely essential to your survival.

Being willing and able to tell a fib is the cornerstone of the art of mingling, the basis from which all the techniques in this book are taught.

Please don't get me wrong. Most of the time, I am a very truthful, direct, and honest person. But light-hearted socializing is by nature a game in which your *primary* goal is to have a good time, not to tell the truth. If you want to succeed at any game, you have to play it. And remember, the lies you are telling are tiny, unimportant social untruths, such as "I have to make a telephone call." The reason for the lie is almost always to keep from hurting someone's feelings, or to smooth over some tension or unpleasantness—not just for your own comfort, but for the comfort of people around you. In other words, being dishonest in mingling is Justifiable Lying, a necessary part of civilization. Perhaps some day we will all be able to tell the truth to each other without causing pain, but as things stand now, lying is usually kinder than telling the absolute truth. And between honesty and kindness, I'll take the latter.

I don't mean to say, however, that minglers lie only to help other people. Certainly not. We're talking about survival here, after all. You're on the mingling battlefield, facing impossible odds, fierce opposition, near calamity. You never know what you'll be asked to handle as a mingler. And while your course of action may or may not call for a friendly fib, it's important to know from the start that when the moment of truth arrives, you may have to . . . lie or die.

DEALING WITH FAUX PAS

We've all made embarrassing errors while mingling; I've made some doozies myself. And yet, each time it happens, each time we're faced with that excruciating moment right after the faux pas when we wish we could just disappear into

the floorboards, we're convinced that no one has ever been so stupid or so clumsy before.

How many times has the following happened to you?

- Calling someone you know by the wrong name
- Spilling something on someone
- Being overheard gossiping about a person, by that person
- Bumping into someone or hurting them in some other physical way
- Bringing up a subject you immediately realize had been a secret
- Talking about last night's great party to which persons present weren't invited
- Loudly mistaking someone's wife or husband for their daughter or son

Whether you've just stepped on someone's foot with your spiked heel or inquired as to the whereabouts of someone's dead husband, try to remember two things: Everyone makes faux pas, even the person to whom you've just done the damage; and there's always a way to recover (at least partially) from any snafu, and to make the best of a bad situation. The important thing is not to fold under the pressure of your social blunder, but to deal with it and learn from it. Faux pas build mingling character, and if you don't run away from them, they can help to make you a much stronger conversationalist.

• When You're Dressed Wrong •

If you've ever walked into a room full of tuxedos and evening gowns in a tweed skirt and knee-highs, as I have, you have experienced the particular vise of horror that grips you when you realize you're dressed all wrong for the party. I'm not talking here about having on a turtleneck instead of a tie—I mean when you are dressed noticeably, definitely *wrong*.

When you find yourself in this situation, you have several choices. **Please note:** I am assuming here that the fact that you're dressed wrong *bothers* you; naturally, if you are either confident enough or enlightened enough not to care, you won't think of this as a faux pas and the following advice doesn't apply.

You can, of course, leave. Turn right around and walk out, rent a movie, and spend a quiet night at home, convinced, it was fate and you would have had a lousy time anyway. But I emphatically *do not* condone this course of action. It's giving up.

Your second option is to go home and change into an appropriate outfit. If you think you can pull this off, by all means, go ahead. But then you have to get out before anybody sees you, or your "Before" and "After" show might be more embarrassing than merely being dressed wrong. Also, the logistics of getting home, changing your clothes, and getting back to the party before it's over may be overwhelming. The nervous stress of going through all that running back and forth may not be worth it. It's bound to put you in a bad mood.

The third choice: Pretend nothing is wrong with the way you are dressed. People with a great deal of poise can carry this off, to a degree. Or people with a great deal of acting ability. In your mind you must see yourself dressed in completely appropriate clothing, then just mingle as you normally would. But don't forget what happened to the emperor in "The Emperor's New Clothes." All it takes is for one person to say to you, "Did you forget this was black tie?" and the illusion could be shattered.

You can also use humor, the universal antidote for faux pas. For instance, if you are in casual clothes and everyone else is in formal dress, you can say in mock amazement, "Look how many people are inappropriately dressed; imagine anyone wearing a tux to an affair like this!" But as always with humor, it has to be funny; if you don't think you can pull it off, don't attempt it.

Your last option, and the one I *do* suggest you choose, is this. *Turn your inappropriate appearance into a mingling story.* This way, you take the hand that's been dealt to you and bluff it out. Imagine you arrive in a gray business suit at your friend Sally's house and, upon entering, you realize everyone is in black tie except for you. Now you remember; the invitation *did* say formal, but you had such a bad day at the office it went right out of your head. But you don't panic. You know that before you begin to mingle, before you talk to anyone, all you have to do is to take the time to decide what your story is going to be. You remain in the coat room for a minute, until you are ready.

You confidently enter the fray. After your opening line, you indicate your attire and say laughingly, "Can you believe this? Ol' Sally really got me this time. She neglected to inform me about black tie. I pulled the same trick on her two years ago and we've been paying each other back ever since." This leads you and the other person into a discussion of practical jokes and of how you both know the hostess. You've successfully turned your inappropriate dress into usable subject matter.

Admittedly, this is a rather bold lie, as it involves fabricating something untrue about the hostess. (And it usually is not a good idea to tell lies about other people.) But Sally, if she *is* a friend of yours, won't mind this innocent ruse, even if she does hear about it, which is highly unlikely. A less outrageous story might be that you have just gotten off a train from somewhere interesting, and didn't have time to go home first. Or you can say that you've been locked out of your apartment, or that the cleaners burned down (along with all your dressy clothes), or that a jealous ex-lover has been stealing all your mail and you never received the actual invitation. Whatever tale you choose to tell, make it intriguing. Remember, your objective is not merely to recover from your fashion faux pas, but to make it work for you, to turn it into a mingling aid, just like wearing an accessory or bringing a prop.

As you can imagine, it's even easier to pull this off if you are overdressed rather than underdressed, like when you're wearing a tux and everyone else is in jeans. Then you simply adopt the position that you are going (or have already gone) to some very fancy, chic affair other than the present one.

A final note about this: Don't forget to consider telling the truth before you decide on a lie. But only if the truth is as interesting as a made-up story would be. If the truth is that you just made a stupid mistake for no particular reason, stick to deceit.

• Introductions: A Recurring Nightmare •

The problem of being awkward with introductions is not, for many, an "unusual situation." You may find that you are often uncertain about whether to introduce someone using their first name, last name, or both; about whether to use a qualifier ("this is my friend, ————"); even about whether or not it is in fact your responsibility to introduce two people in a given situation. But all of this is small potatoes compared with the seemingly inevitable mingling nightmare of having to introduce someone *whose name you have forgotten*.

It's one thing to forget someone's name if you've met them only once or twice, or if you haven't seen them in a while. But all too often it's someone whose name you really should know, and who is going to be insulted to find out you don't. In other words, a faux pas in the making.

This is absolute agony when it happens, and I've watched

111

hundreds of minglers try to deal with it in different ways, ranging from exuberant apology ("Oh GOD, I'm so sorry, JEEZ, wow, I can't *believe* this, I can't *believe* I've forgotten your name!") to throwing up their hands and walking away. But there are better ways to deal with this kind of mental slip. Next time you draw a blank while making introductions, try one of the following ploys:

1. **Force them to introduce themselves.** This is the smoothest and most effective way to handle your memory lapse. When it's done well, no one will ever suspect you. If you have forgotten one person's name in the group, turn to that person first and smile. Then turn invitingly to a person whose name you do remember and say, "This is Linden Bond," turning back casually toward the forgotten person. The person whose name you haven't mentioned yet will automatically (it's a reflex) say, "Nice to meet you, Linden, I'm Sylvia Cooper," and usually offer a hand to shake.

   If you are trying to introduce two people and you can't remember *either* of their names, your problem is more serious. Still you can usually get away with simply saying, "Have you two met each other?" If you smile confidently and wait, the two will introduce themselves (though those few seconds while you're waiting can seem like a lifetime). At the very worst it will appear as if your introduction skills are a bit sloppy, but no one will be able to tell you've forgotten their names.

2. **Confess, then dwell on it.** Here's another example of turning a faux pas to your advantage. What you do is admit you've forgotten the name(s), apologizing sincerely. After the introductions are over, let the mishap lead you into a discussion of why it is harder for some people to remember names than others (the left brain/right brain theory, the male/female theory, etc.). Using your own mingling error as subject matter shows that you are comfortable with your mistake; you don't feel that guilty about it. And since peo-

112

ple tend to believe whatever you project, no one will hold a grudge.

3. **Ask them how they pronounce their name.** Okay, so this is a bit riskier. If the person answers "John," you're a goner.

4. **Introduce them using something besides their name.** Names and labels are highly overrated in our society anyway. Why not say instead, "Jody, I want you to meet a woman after your own heart!" Then you just present the other person, who will offer her name or not. You can also cover up any uneasiness you have about your forgetting names by using flattery: "I want you to meet the most fascinating person at the party!" or "You two should really meet—seeing as how you're both so gorgeous!" If you lay it on thick, it puts up a smoke screen and nobody will notice you've forgotten their names. Or if they do, they won't care anymore!

• Storytelling as a Healing Technique •

Introduction problems are one thing, but what about the really bad faux pas? How can you deal with that horrible, sinking terror that engulfs you right after one of those conversation-stopping social blunders, such as when the hostess overhears you telling someone that the only reason you came to her party was because you had nothing else to do? It's not easy to go on after one of these disasters until you do something to help heal the social wound you've inadvertently inflicted.

Keep in mind that everyone, at one time or another, makes a fool of himself while mingling. In fact, if you never made any mistakes, socially, you'd never improve your mingling skills. Taking risks, at least occasionally, is necessary to your mingling growth—I might even go so far as to say it is necessary to your social health. Since everyone knows what it feels like to make a faux pas, everyone is just as anxious as the one who has committed the social sin to see him recover. They want the tension to pass as much as he does. It is for this reason, I think, that Storytelling is such an effective way of mending the mingling faux pas.

The first thing you need for this technique is a really good faux pas story. The idea is to tell the witnesses of your current faux pas about something you did at another time that was more embarrassing than whatever it is you have just done. Ideally, it should be something that actually happened to you or to someone you know, because in the wake of whatever terrible social error you've committed, you have to be open and sincere in order to reestablish your position in the group. If told well, your story will dispel the humiliation surrounding you.

I confess I make faux pas often, especially while trying out new lines and maneuvers, but I have a great faux pas story—a true one—which almost always acts as a healing ointment for any mistakes I may have made. What I usually do, in the midst of the embarrassing silence or the nervous laughter I have caused, is to say something like, "I really can't believe I just did that (said that). Boy, leave it to me! Did I ever tell you about the time I . . ." And I recount my Erica Jong story.

Years ago when I was looking for a job, someone had arranged for me to have an interview with Erica Jong, for the position of her secretarial assistant. At that time I was very nervous to be meeting a famous author, and it didn't help that I had broken my foot and was on crutches. On top of everything else, the evening of the interview it was raining and I couldn't get a cab. By the time I arrived at Ms. Jong's Upper East Side townhouse—my hair dripping wet, dragging my muddy crutches—I was almost an hour late for the interview. I was a complete wreck. What a way to begin! But I took a deep breath and rang the doorbell.

The housekeeper let me in, and then the fabulous Erica Jong herself came sweeping down the front stairs. She graciously put out her hand.

"Hello, I'm Erica Jong," she said to me, smiling.

I looked straight into her eyes, smiled back at her and said, "Hello, I'm Erica Jong."

(!)

In my nervousness and general disarray, I had actually introduced myself as her! There was a long, long moment of the loudest silence I have ever experienced—everybody, I think, was totally confused—until Ms. Jong came through for both of us like the mingling pro she must be, and reminded me gently,

"You must be Jeanne Martinet."

"Uh . . . yes, that's who I am," I agreed sheepishly.

I don't think there are many moments (certainly I haven't had many) in life that can rival the embarrassment of the one I just described; however, the incident did end up serving a very useful purpose: it gets me out of faux pas hot water almost every time. After I tell that story, no one thinks too much about whatever current error I may have committed.

When using a personal anecdote as a healing tool, remember: It is better if you are the faux pas *perpetrator* in the tale you tell; it's not as effective to tell a story about someone else messing up. It can sound as if you are trying to compare your faux pas favorably to someone else's. (Although, if the story is outstanding in some way, it can work.) Also, you can use storytelling to help someone else recover from a faux pas ("Hey, don't worry about it; let me tell you about the time I . . ."). This is the ultimate mingling move: In one fell swoop you've been kind to a fellow human being, endeared yourself to him or her for at least the remainder of the party, taken control of the conversation, and found a reason to tell one of your favorite stories!

Disclaimer: Storytelling won't work in every situation, of course. If you've just spilled hot coffee on someone's blouse, that person is probably not going to stick around while you tell a story.

• Quick Recovery Lines •

If you don't have a good story to tell or if the type of error you are guilty of making doesn't allow for storytelling, you may be able to use one of the recovery lines below to regain your balance. Quick Recovery Lines are also invaluable to the many people who are so paralyzed after a faux pas that a short line or two is all they are able to utter.

"Just testing."

"Sorry, it's a line I read somewhere."

"Did I say that out loud?"

"Let's run that scene over."

"Okay. So I need a few lessons in mingling."

"I'm on automatic pilot tonight, and I think I just crashed!"

"Excuse me. Another personality took over my body there for a minute."

"Um, is there a time machine anywhere around?"

"Forgive me, I'm afraid I'm not feeling at all well."

"I'm terribly sorry, I'm afraid your beauty has short-circuited me."

"Arrggh! Somebody up there must hate me!"

"I always wondered what would happen if I ever really embarrassed myself . . . I'm still alive. Good."

"That was my evil twin, Skippy."

NEGOTIATING TOUGH ROOMS

Every time you set out to go to a party, you are entering the world of the Unknown. It's important to be prepared for any scenario—to be ready to adapt the basic rules of mingling to fit—as you have no idea what may greet you once you get there.

116

• The Sardine Can •

Sometimes you are faced with what I like to call the Sardine Can. You arrive at a social function and discover it's wall-to-wall people. You hesitate at the door before going in; it seems like masochism to try to mingle in this teeming mass of humanity. You know that movement will be limited, fresh air scarce, and the line for the bathroom impossibly long. But for some crazy reason, you go in anyway. (I know I always do.)

Since you've elected to become a sardine, here are some helpful tips on how best to proceed:

1. **Use the most direct openings and subject matter in your mingling portfolio.** Crowded parties are invariably loud, so any kind of complicated communication is out. Forget trying anything that entails irony or nuance, for example. People aren't going to be able to hear you. And the Fade-in approach is definitely out. I recommend the Honest Approach as an entrance maneuver for the Sardine Can; people are more or less resigned to the fact that since they can't move, they have to talk to whomever happens to be next to them. For this reason, you'll find it easier than usual to get into conversations. It's just hard to *have* them, in all the din!

2. **Keep your eye out for anyone close to you who is making her way through the crowd.** Think of boxcar riding. When a train passes by, jump on! This is your only hope of movement at a really packed party. If someone is strong enough or determined enough to wade through the multitude, take advantage of the path she is cutting and follow in her wake. You don't even have to know exactly where you are going; between the food, the bar, and the bathroom, you're bound to get closer to somewhere you want to be! This maneuver is much more extreme than Piggybacking; here, it's okay if you actually hang on to the person (as long as they don't mind). They probably won't

117

even notice. When I see people doing this well, it reminds me of how New York City taxis use a speeding ambulance to get through a traffic jam.

3. **Don't worry about escape techniques.** While actual, physical movement may be limited, it's much easier to exit, psychologically speaking. The Sardine Can is a much more informal place, due to the decreased personal space. Rules of courtesy and etiquette are relaxed. Really crowded parties are so chaotic anyway that people will hardly notice when you walk away from them. And even if you should happen to be in a one-on-one with an obnoxious type who doesn't want to let you go, you won't lack for human sacrifices. Just reach out and grab someone, and hook him up with your leech.

4. **Smile a lot.** Facial expressions of all kinds are at a premium while you are in the Sardine Can. Since hearing is limited, body language has to take the place of verbal communication. (In fact, a working knowledge of sign language could be a plus.)

• The Thin Room •

It's a whole different kettle of fish when you arrive at an affair and find that there is practically no one there. It could just be that you're early, in which case it's only a temporary Thin Room and you can wait it out. But if it's already an hour and a half after the party's official starting time, those five or six guests could be it. And the rules of human kindness dictate that you remain—at least for a little while—since the hostess may be suicidal at this point. (She's not about to let you get away in any case; she's probably locked the door after you.)

Here are some suggestions about how to handle the Thin Room:

1. **Encourage togetherness.** Probably the best time that can be had by all is if everyone stops trying to pretend it's a normal mingling situation. If there are only five people

there, give up the structure of a cocktail party (where people are supposed to stand up and mingle) and help the hostess turn it into an intimate soirée instead (sit in chairs and on the sofa in a cozy circle). But you should at least try to maneuver any separate groups closer together, for the simple reason that it is going to make it much easier for you to move between them. If you have a group of two people on one side of the room and a group of three way over on the other, it's going to be awkward to circulate. Having to walk by yourself across an empty room can make you self-conscious.

2. **Offer to get people things.** The fewer people there are, the more energy is needed to create a fun atmosphere. Help the hostess by making sure the few guests who are there are as happy as they can be. Your ulterior motive: volunteering to assist the host gives you more freedom to move around quickly. In the Thin Room it's essential that you not get stuck with a Dud or a Bore for a long time—you could end up being the last two living souls at the party. The Thin Room can become the Empty Room in a blink of an eye.

3. **Use Playing a Game as much as possible.** Game playing (see Chapter 2) can really help pep up a party. You should never, of course, suggest playing an actual party game like Charades or Dictionary without the express approval and encouragement of the hostess. Although, in the old days, nothing saved a Thin Room so much as a good game of Twister.

4. **Bolster your hostess.** You may be disappointed that there aren't more people at the party, but just think how your hostess feels, if people she invited didn't show. Since you can't do anything about the fact that this is a Thin Room, take this opportunity to make your hostess feel good about her party. Flatter the food, praise the decorations; tell her

you feel lucky to have her a little more to yourself for once. In the Thin Room, it's vital that you project the positive. Everyone will appreciate it.

• Mingling with Drunks •

In almost every etiquette book ever written, from the early 1900s on, there is a section, usually written for the benefit of young ladies, on the proper and safe way to handle their inebriated gentlemen friends. Alice Leone Moats, in her famous 1935 *No Nice Girl Swears,* went so far as to categorize the different kinds of drunks: hilarious, lachrymose, loquacious, taciturn, argumentative, magisterial, belligerent, sentimental, amorous, and vomitous.

I don't know whether it's my age, the times, or the social circle I'm in, but I rarely run into anything but the more benign type of drunk—the hilarious, the loquacious, and the sentimental—all of which, depending on the level of inebriation, are easy to deal with—even amusing, sometimes. However, if you do happen to find yourself up against one of the more unpleasant species of drunks, here are some guidelines.

1. **Never argue with a drunk.** It's useless. Humor the drunk, as you would a crazy person. But don't encourage him either. If he says he is strong enough to lift you over his head, agree that he is certainly strong enough, but do not give him the opportunity to try it.

2. **Never flirt with a drunk.** You may as well play with matches near an open tub of gasoline. And I am talking about women drunks as well as men.

3. **Never tell a drunk you think he or she is drunk.** Unless he's your friend, and even then it's best to wait until morning to discuss the evils of alcohol.

4. **Remember that you don't have to mingle with a drunk unless you choose to.** It's the easiest thing in the world, usually, to escape from real drunks. Their senses are

so dull that you can use any escape technique you want and they'll never know what hit them. A lot of people seem to forget this and allow boring drunks to corner them for long periods of time. Don't buy into the drunk's illusion that he is in control, mingling-wise (or any other wise) A simple "excuse me," and a hasty retreat is fine. Don't worry about leaving him standing all alone; he'll find someone else quickly enough. And if you use the Human Sacrifice exit technique to escape from your drunk, try to find another drunk and sic them on each other. Otherwise, you could end up making enemies. Making enemies will not help you in mastering the art of mingling!

5. **If the drunk is really offensive, you can use the experience to your advantage at the party.** Remember the Helpless Hannah Ploy (page 41), in which you asked people for help in order to have something to talk about? When you are being bothered by a heavy-duty drunk, you can have any number of people protecting you from the drunk, whether you are male or female. Remember the old Chinese proverb: Once someone saves your life, they are responsible for it forever. (Translation: Once someone saves you from a drunk, they've basically adopted you and will have to welcome you into whatever group they may be in later.)

6. **Warn your host about a bad drunk.** By "bad drunk" I mean someone who is getting violent, or who is unsteady enough to damage property. "Live and let live" is a good philosophy, in most cases; after all, you are there to mingle, not to be a policeman. But it's nice to alert the host to a potential problem, so that he can decide whether or not he wants to try to do anything about it.

One last piece of advice on this subject. If there are a *lot* of drunks at the party, cut your mingling short and go home. Or go straight to the bar and order a triple martini.

• Mingling Among Minglephobics •

Almost everyone has minglephobia, to some degree. But what do you do when you are at a party with a lot of extreme minglephobics, or are in a one-on-one mingling situation with someone who is very shy and socially self-conscious?

You can tell something is wrong when you deliver your top three sure-fire lines—the ones that never fail—and they all fall flat. When all you get is silence or monosyllabic responses, you can be pretty sure it's a case of minglephobia.

First: Realize there's nothing wrong with *you*. This is very important, because minglephobia is a contagious disease. Say it in your head like a mantra, if it will help: "It's not me . . . It's not me."

Second: Use an interview style with the minglephobic. You're going to have to try to draw him out. Pretend you're Barbara Walters and he's Warren Beatty. Ask lots of questions—preferably questions that require more than a yes or no answer. The best questions for drawing out a shy person are questions involving superlatives, such as "What's the biggest tip you ever got?" or "Who was your most difficult client?" Have your next question ready as soon as the first one is out of your mouth; his answers are not bound to be very lengthy. As you ask the questions, watch his face carefully for any signs of life. If you see a flicker, you may have hit upon a conversational "hot spot," and you will want to pursue that line of questioning.

Third: If interviewing the minglephobic doesn't work, or if you get tired of it, try flattering him. It's always a good idea when dealing with insecure people to flatter them, especially in areas where they may feel the weakest. So say to the minglephobic, "I don't meet that many people I enjoy talking to as much as you." If they don't open up after that one, then you've done your best and it may be time to move on. Remember, minglephobics will drain you of your energy, because you will be doing the mingling for both of you. Don't let them sap your strength.

If the whole party is filled with minglephobics, you'd better have eaten your Wheaties that morning!

• Mingling with the Truly Arrogant •

For nearly all of the many social situations one can imagine, my advice is to try to be as positive and friendly as possible. But when mingling with the Truly Arrogant, there is only one path open to you: *Be tough and treat 'em rough!*

Truly Arrogant people usually travel in packs, so you'll probably have to deal with them in a group rather than just one here or there. They can be country-club types, fashion designers, media people, or just the very rich. But in any case, they are hard to approach and often say things like, "You must be absolutely thrilled to be here, darling. Can I explain any of the hors d'oeuvres to you?"

Of course, if you have any sense and you have the option, you should just go home. Truly Arrogant people are no fun to play with. But sometimes, for whatever reasons, you're forced to stay and make the best of it. Perhaps it's a business party and you're obligated to mingle; perhaps you're with a date and you don't want to make her leave. But whatever the reason, it may help if you remember a few simple rules for Mingling with the Truly Arrogant:

1. **Make use of the Survival Fantasies.** If there is ever a time to use them, this is it. Mingling with the Truly Arrogant requires confidence. (See page 3.)

2. **Breathe deeply.** This is always a good idea. It will help you to relax.

3. **Try not to flatter them.** Your first inclination will be to try to win them over by being overly nice. But Truly Arrogant people are usually conceited, and conceited people don't really respect flattery. In any case, flattery will give too much power to someone who is already assuming superiority.

4. **Gently insult the Truly Arrogant.** You have to try to communicate with them on their level first; show them you speak their language. Be careful, however. Your goal is bantering, not battering. It should be more of a teasing than serious insulting. And this works best if you are dealing with the opposite sex. Tell him you've heard something terrible about him, or if he's a celebrity, pretend you've never heard of him (or confuse him with some other celebrity who doesn't look at all like him). You've got to come on strong with these power mongers, and never let them see that it matters to you whether they like you or not.

However, once the Truly Arrogant person starts to warm up to you, once he begins to drop his snooty attitude, you must reward him by relenting and being nice to him. The rules for Mingling with the Truly Arrogant apply *only for as long as the person exhibits his arrogant behavior.*

THE SIT-DOWN MINGLE

This section will not cover the rules of sit-down dinners, as those occasions, while usually pleasant, do not fall under the category of mingling. What I'm talking about here are those times when you are at a large party and you make the fateful decision to sit down.

There are several reasons for sitting down at a party where most people are standing up. Either your feet are tired (an excellent reason); you want to escape from someone, so you *pretend* your feet are tired (better make sure there's no space available next to you on the sofa); you've taken a heap of food from the buffet and are having trouble eating it while standing; or you would like to have a one-on-one conversation with someone without being interrupted. All these are good reasons for taking a load off. But you should also be aware of the dangers of sitting.

The scariest thing about the Sit-Down Mingle is how difficult it can be to get back up. It is very hard to execute exit maneuvers from a sitting-down position. You could inadvertently sit next to a Venus Flytrap, someone who has been just sitting there, waiting for someone to sit down next to her so she can tell them all about her recent gall bladder operation. Even if you sit down next to someone you know you'd love to talk to, that person could get up shortly after you've sat down, leaving you feeling publicly abandoned and more important, leaving you wide open to the person you may have sat down to escape! You take a big risk when you sit down, so make sure it's really where you want to be.

The other, more insidious danger is a purely psychological one; once you are sitting down, you may lose your mingling momentum. You may find yourself thinking, "This is such a comfortable chair; maybe I'll just watch. What's so great about talking to people anyway?" WARNING! If you feel yourself slipping into this state of minglephobia, get up! *Immediately!*

In order to master the Sit-Down Mingle, you have to learn how to get back on your feet. It's extremely hard to get free of someone (the Venus Flytrap, for example) who is really talking *at* you while you are both sitting down. She's basically got you where she wants you; you are her prisoner, or at least that's how it can feel to you.

Many of the normal escape techniques are problematic to perform from a sitting position; however, there are a couple techniques that I have found work pretty well. The first is a version of the Buffet Bye-Bye and Other Handy Excuses (see page 67). Here, an excuse you can use is the exact opposite of the one you probably used to sit down in the first place: you interrupt the person and say, "I'm sorry, but I have *got* to stand up. If I don't get up now, I never will." In the more polite form of this, you ask the Flytrap if she would like to stand up with you. If she says yes, then once you have her on her feet, you can use the Human Sacrifice (page 65) or any number of other escape tactics to shake her off.

The Human Sacrifice also can be done from a sitting-down position, in this manner: Find someone nearby and get his attention. Try to bring him into the conversation a little; toss a comment up at him, include him in whatever it is the Flytrap is talking about. The minute the new person even smiles at something you or the Flytrap says, start to get up, indicate your place and say, "Would you care for a seat?" Now, depending on his aspect as you stand, you may want to use the more aggressive, "Would you save my seat for a second?" This is a bit wicked, because it's almost impossible for a new person to refuse, but as I've said before, all's fair in love and mingling. (Of course, you *don't* come back. In fact, try not to be visible to that side of the room.) The Human Sacrifice from a chair is definitely a bold move to make but at the worst, it's clunky. It will *always* get you out of your seat, even if the Flytrap comes with you. Once you've begun your ascent, you can't be stopped.

One final word about the Sit-Down Mingle. Don't try it if you are tipsy or tired. There's only one thing I know of that's more impolite than getting drunk at a party and that's falling asleep. Especially if you snore (horrors!).

QUICK-FIXES FOR DIRE CIRCUMSTANCES

• How to React to Hand-Kissing and Other Physicalities •

On occasion, someone will get physical with you in a way that makes you feel uncomfortable—a kiss on the hand, an arm around the waist, a pat on the head, a kiss on the back of the neck (once, someone even pulled on my ear, I swear)—and you are not going to know what to do or say.

Every person's sense of physical boundaries is different. Some people can accept a hug or a kiss from a perfect stranger, while others see this as an almost criminal invasion of their personal space. Even hand-kissing is considered the height of chivalry by some and the height of insolence by others. For most people however, when someone gets physical, it at least calls for some kind of comment. Whether you are flattered, embarrassed, or insulted, one of the lines below may come in handy. They are listed in order of most positive (that was very nice) to most negative (try that again and I'll brain you).

"Why, thank you kindly, Sir (Madam)!"

"Chivalry is alive!"

"Enchanté, monsieur."

"I'm not that kind of girl!" (Use this even if you are male)

"Must you do that?"

"Was that absolutely necessary?"

"Don't touch unless you're buying."

"Have you had your shots?"

"Excuse me, nobody informed me we had become intimate."

"Hey! I'm not silly putty, you know!"

"Sorry, babe, you're on private property."

"What do I look like to you—a grapefruit?" (Use only for hugs, squeezes, or pinches)

• Handling Insults •

The best story I ever heard about handling insults came from a friend of mine. I'll call him Tony (the name has been changed, for reasons that will be clear). It seems Tony was at a party where he was discussing a film he had just seen, when a man who had been listening suddenly challenged him.

"You don't really mean to say you *enjoyed* that piece of garbage?" the man said to him in a snide voice. Startled, Tony tried to defend himself.

"Well, . . . I mean it's not that I think it's great *art* or anything, but I thought it was entertaining, yes."

The man sneered. "Well, why would anybody in the film industry bother to make great *art*," the man said, "as long as there's pea-brains like you out there?"

Tony was absolutely stunned at the nastiness of this man, as were the other people within hearing distance. The insult had been so vicious, and so uncalled for, that Tony felt there was no way to respond to him—verbally.

But Tony has his own method—a *non*verbal one—of dealing with this kind of thing. He waited a little while, then located the drunkest person at the party and took him aside for a few minutes. Not too long after that, there was an unfortunate "accident." Tony had paid the drunk five dollars to spill his drink on the man who had insulted him!

Putting a contract out on someone at a party may not be your style, and certainly most insults are much less aggressive than the one Tony experienced. Also, most of the time, you are going to have witnesses to the insult and you will feel the need to respond right away to earn or keep the respect of the others around you. So usually, the best way to handle someone who has insulted you is to hit them immediately with a snappy comeback like the ones below. As you can see, they range from the corny (which can diffuse a tense situation) to the biting (which may be more satisfying to use). Feel free to record your own preferred "backlashes" in the space provided. **Warning:** Make sure you've actually been insulted before using any of these lines. They are only for self-defense!

"I'd hate to have your nerve in a tooth."

"I wouldn't want to take a bite out of you—you're a cookie full of arsenic."

"Are you this mean to everybody, or am I just lucky?"

"What charm school are you a graduate of?"

"My mother always said I shouldn't talk to strangers; now I know why!"

"I know what's really bothering you. But don't worry, you can't even tell that's a toupé from across the room."

"My, that looks painful. (What?) Your face."

"If I had an eraser, I'd rub you out."

"Are you a good witch, or a bad witch?"

"Your mind is poisoned. Why don't you let it spread to the rest of your body?"

"_____"

"_____"

"_____"

• All-Purpose Lines for Treating Panic •

Having supplied all sorts of detailed advice and instructions for every conceivable set of circumstances, I do recognize that there are times when many people simply feel general mingler's panic. You may be terrified because you've suddenly realized you don't understand what is being said to you; you

129

may be confused or feel you have lost your place in a conversation (and can't remember the Dot-dot-dot Plot). You may suspect you've been insulted but just aren't sure. You may have a blind urge to run and don't even know why. Well, don't worry. There are a few simple lines that—while they're not very sophisticated—can save you when you are suffering from a panic attack. When you feel that freezing terror hit you, try to gauge the atmosphere you're in and pick the most appropriate of these lines:

"You know, I love your voice."

"I'm dizzy. Is it hot in here?"

"What you say makes sense."

"Hmm. Life is interesting."

• Cutting Your Losses
(or, When to Just Give Up and Leave) •

The best poker players know when to fold. No matter how much skill you have or how much desire to play the game, sometimes it's simply not in the cards for you to mingle. Sometimes you can tell after only ten minutes that you should never have come to the particular function on that particular night. If you stay, you are going to end up having a bad time and—what's worse—it's going to be bad for your self-image, because you are apt to perform badly. So if you're too tired, too sick, or too distracted to put the right amount of energy into the experience of being at a party, realize this quickly and act on it. In other words, cut your losses and go home.

Make very certain, however, that you are not throwing in the towel simply because you are *afraid* to mingle. Many people pose as introverts who can't be bothered with socializing when actually it's because they're all frozen up with terror inside. Learning to recognize your own minglephobia is an important step in learning and mastering the art of mingling.

If you do end up calling it quits on occasion, don't let the experience keep you from welcoming future mingling opportunities. Everybody skips a party now and then. But always remember that every new gathering—like every human being—is totally unique and unpredictable. You don't want to risk missing what may turn out to be the best time you ever had.

·7·

NEW TECHNOLOGIES: MINGLING IN THE NINETIES

Topics and Buzzwords for the New Decade

T he smartest minglers are knowledgeable about the issues and trends of the day, so that when they hear them mentioned at parties, they will understand something of what is being said. Unlike most conversation experts, however, I do *not* advise you to tear desperately through newspapers and magazines right before the party, so you'll be "up" on current events. My feeling is, you're either tuned into the world around you, or you're not. No amount of last-minute cramming is going to make you a better-informed person.

Although you may want to familiarize yourself with the following "nineties" topics and buzzwords, don't run to the library to do research on the ones you are uncertain about. Just be aware that these are things that are "in the air," and keep an ear out for them in your everyday life—and as you read, listen to, or watch the news. Then the next time somebody at a party tosses out the term "virtual reality," for example, you will be able to contribute something instead of just standing there with a blank look on your face, wondering how you can change the subject to fishing or something else you know about.

Please note: Make sure you have correctly heard the topic before you jump into the conversation. I once had an extremely bizarre fifteen-minute discussion with a friend about croquet—until we both realized that *he* had been talking about cocaine!

• NINETIES TOPICS •

adult education
animal rights
abstinence
baby selling
biotechnology
brain mapping
breast implants
bungee jumping
cellular phones
CD-ROM
cold fusion
computer bulletin boards
computer viruses
crystals
the Chunnel
DAT (digital audio tape)
E-mail (electronic mail)
earthquake protection
environmental issues
fiber optics
generation X
grandparents' visitation rights

the homeless
integrative technology
laser discs
low-rub ink
lounge acts
men's groups
multiculturalism
nanotechnology
Native Americans
the ozone holes
pesticide-resistant insects
rain forests
robotics
rollerblades
recycling
saloning
shadism
silicone implants
sexual harassment
stereoscopic X-ray
substance-free college dormitories

the greenhouse effect
HDTV (high-definition tele-
vision)
health insurance
herbal medicine, homeopathy

supercomputers
synergy
ultraviolet rays
Velcro wall-jumping
virtual reality

• NINETIES BUZZWORDS/SLANG •

Slang is like fashion; by the time you figure out how to use it, it's out of style. But here are some of the "in" terms being used now. I have provided space for you to record the lastest, if you want (better use pencil!). If you hear a new word that people seem to be using, ask someone right then and there what it means. If you are too embarrassed to admit your ignorance, take an in-the-know friend aside later and ask him.

Word or phrase	Meaning
. . . *not!*	Strong, sarcastic negative ("You sure are intelligent . . . *not!*")
beast	an attractive woman
fly	an attractive woman
butt soup	someone in an ugly outfit
fake bake	a tanning salon tan
home boy	a person from the same neighborhood
chronologically challenged	old
vertically challenged	short
mint	the greatest; best
random	cool in an unexpected way
dope	cool, hip
fossil	person who has been a college student for more than four years
crushed	destroyed, as in "he destroyed me"

bugging	going crazy
the hyperlost generation	today's generation
channel surfing	scanning TV channels with the remote control
PC	politically correct
Magoo	an old man who drives slowly
tongue-knot	a couple kissing for a very long time
lifejacket	condom
the whole guy	the entire thing
on the beach	unemployed
to be layered	to be given lesser duties and a different job title
in the hurt box	in trouble
green	environmentally conscious
to greenlight	to give the go ahead, approve
squirrel chasers	cross–country skiers
shingle mingle	a party on the roof

THE DANGERS OF TALKING POLITICS

We've all heard the old adage a million times: Never talk politics or religion at a social gathering. Our mothers drummed it into our heads, as did their mothers with them. The assumption is that these are two areas people feel very strongly about and which aren't subject to normal rules of logic and pleasant debate. People tend to disagree—especially when it comes to politics—in a more disagreeable manner than they do at any other time. And most people will admit that while a difference of opinion can be stimulating, yelling and name-calling can really wreck a party.

Also, when you are at a large party, you are supposed to be

mingling, ideally. That is, having conversations that are brief and plentiful. Once you start talking about next year's election, you're liable to forget all about circulating. But by far the most serious danger is the emotional one; most people, when talking politics, reach their boiling point quickly and find themselves saying things they hadn't planned on saying. When two or more guests start arguing, it can cause a kind of air bubble at the party; people nearby will turn and stare, or worse, join in—and then your discussion can become an interference in everyone's mingling pleasure. (Like the time Uncle Henry ruined the Christmas party when he got into a political argument and ended up by throwing the turkey at Mr. Baker, yelling that bird brains should stick together.)

The dangers of talking politics are as real as ever, but get ready for a shock, because I believe it's about time we rewrote the time-honored golden rule to read: It's *okay* to talk politics and religion, just don't *argue violently* about politics and religion.

Let's face it. Our lives are too closely connected with politics to avoid the subject entirely. With governments crumbling right and left (no pun intended), the planet in critical condition, our economy in a recession (or depression, depending on whom you talk to), how can intelligent people gathered together for conversation totally avoid the subject of politics? It's gotten so that if you are wearing a fur hat or a leather belt, or if you mention you attended the now highly controversial Columbus Day parade, you are making a political statement, of one kind or another. The nineties *is* politics.

In any case, I suspect the old rule stemmed at least partially from the fact that women in the past were not supposed to have anything in their pretty little heads to discuss politics *with.* (Weren't the men always retiring to the library in the old movies, to smoke cigars and drink port and talk about "serious matters"?) It was not considered polite for men to talk about such things in *mixed company,* lest the ladies be excluded from the discussion.

And so, though mingling is for the most part supposed to be a light-hearted affair, mingling in the nineties is bound to be a little less superficial. After all, what would be the point of mingling if all we ever talked about was the color of the drapes? Talking politics has its minefields, but it can be worth it for the interesting conversations you can end up having. However, you do have to know how to negotiate your way through the dangers. (I am not going to differentiate between religion and politics because they are so closely intertwined. The rules for handling religion are the same as below; however, I have found in general that religion is a less volatile area. The most dangerous subject you could choose spans *both* politics and religion: abortion).

1. **Know your own boiling point.** *This is extremely important.* You have to be certain that you can recognize that moment when you are about to go over the edge into anger—a very hard thing to pinpoint when you are in the middle of talking about the welfare system—and stop. It's a bit like trying to stop drinking before you get drunk; when the moment comes, you can't relate to why you decided to stop in the first place. But I reiterate: If you don't think you can do this (or if all your friends tell you you can't) then go back to the original rule. Don't talk politics.

2. **Test for fanaticism.** Even if you are capable in most circumstances of keeping your head, you have to be very careful with *whom* you talk politics. While it takes two to argue, I don't know many people who can stay serene when confronted with a fanatic. To help you spot one before it's too late, you should develop some "test questions" to administer to the person. You can analyze his or her response to decide if you think the water is safe. Keep a close watch on facial expression; it can tell you more than verbal response. The test lines below are just suggestions; this testing device, more than any other, requires your own personal touch. **Warning:** These tests are never foolproof. People's belief systems are not always as straightforward as you expect.

137

"What newspaper do you like to read?"

"I just bumped into someone who looked exactly like [name of current political figure]."

"I bet they don't eat much better than this in the White House!"

"Last night I had a dream about the President!"

3. **Be a diplomat.** Imagine that you're a foreign diplomat at an international cocktail party. Try to remain impersonal and cool, with observations such as "Well, our economy sure isn't doing too well now," rather than "Are you trying to tell me that we're not in desperate trouble economically?!" A good rule of thumb is to avoid asking questions (unless they are truly informational, such as "Have you read about the bill Congress just passed?"), and don't let your voice get any louder or faster than it would be if you were talking about dessert.

4. **Learn how to defuse and escape.** The minute you feel yourself losing control, or when you realize your partner in political dispute has lost it, *defuse and/or escape.* This is not beginner stuff, here. Once again, you have to *want* to stop. (Breathing deeply may help, as will moving to another place in the room, or getting somebody else to join both of you. Remember: *change equals movement; movement equals change.*) Here are some examples of some lines you can use either to defuse the situation and go on talking about something else (not that likely, if one of you is in emotional overdrive) or to defuse and escape:

"Well, I don't know about that, but there's one thing I do know about: I'm hungry! Will you excuse me?"

"Well, I guess we can't solve the world's problems in one night."

"Listen to us arguing! No wonder my mother always told me never to talk politics at a party! Do you want to get a drink?"

(jokingly) *"Well, I guess we'd better talk about something else or step outside!"*

The most important thing to remember when you decide to talk politics is your mingling objective (the one that should override all others): You are there to have a good time, not to solve the world's problems or change anybody's mind (which you can't do anyway). So, shake hands and come out NOT fighting.

THE SINGLES MINGLE

What if, far from looking for an argument, you are mingling for love? Or perhaps you are at a party for another reason, but you happen to meet that certain someone who sets your heart a-thumping?

If you're seriously on the prowl for romance, you're going to need the most up-to-date love lines. The lines used in today's sexual minuet are a bit different than the ones used in the seventies and eighties. On the other hand, does anything in birds and bees territory ever really change?

Old line: *"Haven't we met somewhere before?"*
90s line: *"I think I know you from a past life."*

Old line: *"You have the most extraordinary green eyes!"*
90s line: *"You have the most extraordinary green hair!"*

Old line: *"I really like your smile."*
90s line: *"I really like your energy."*

Old line: *"Are you married?"*
90s line: *"Are you married, gay, or sexually confused?"*

Old line: *"Did anyone ever tell you you were beautiful?"*
90s line: *"Did anyone ever tell you you have a beautiful aura?"*

Old line: *"My name is Richard, but you can call me Rickie."*
90s line: *"My name is Richard, but you can call me Eagle-With-Long-Claws"*

Old line: *"What's your sign?"*
90s line: *"What's my sign?"*

Old line: *"Your place or mine?"*
90s line: *"Your parents' place or mine?"*

One other piece of advice about today's Singles Mingle: Whether you are mingling at the health club, a self-help workshop, a convention, or a good old-fashioned cocktail party, try not to limit your mingling to "prospects." Your aim should always be to meet as many people as possible. You never know where your "dream" man or woman is going to come from; it could end up being the brother or sister of someone you meet at tonight's party. The more connections you make, the better. Of course, there's no rule against going back to have a second or third chat with someone you're attracted to. But unless you fall madly in love, circulate. He (she)'ll be more intrigued if you don't stick like glue.

If you *should* happen to meet your soul mate, and fall in love at first sight, complete with bells and fireworks, by all means . . . stop mingling!

NEW FRONTIERS: WHERE NO ONE HAS GONE BEFORE

• Lines on Line •

It seems as though we are spending more and more time waiting in long lines: store check-out lines, ticket lines, restaurant lines, lines at the bank or post office, movie lines—and the most daunting and torturous line of all: the line for the ladies' room. Long lines can be tiring, frustrating, and boring—a real waste of time. But they don't have to be. Because almost every one of those tedious experiences can be turned into a mingling event!

Think about it. You've got all those people, standing together not talking to each other, for the most part; and they already have one thing in common: whatever you are standing in line for. That's more of a beginning than you have at many parties, where sometimes the only thing you have in common is the host. You never know what interesting people you may meet if you just take the initiative.

I would not say that mingling while on line is easy; there are many obstacles, not least being the very fact of the line itself. You are basically trying to mingle without the use of your legs. Many techniques—escape, for example—are drastically different when you are in a line. You have to overcome people's natural suspicion of you (a lot of people are uncomfortable if a stranger starts talking to them), plus you must be prepared for your conversation to be overheard by the entire line. When you mingle in a line, you are usually conversing *directly* with only one or two people, but you are almost *performing* for a large group—who, because they are not at an official mingling function, feel no compunction about just standing around watching.

However, mingling in lines can be very rewarding—if somewhat challenging—and since you will probably never see any of these people again (famous last words!), it's relatively risk free. Here are some specific rules and sample lines for the various on-line mingles (an * signifies that the line is generic; it can be used for any of the situations):

Check-out lines: People in check-out lines can be tough customers, depending on what they are purchasing. Many people put their personal armor on when they are buying. If what they've got in their basket or cart looks a bit strange to you, don't mention it. You're going to have to be very non-threatening and incredibly nice when you deliver your opening

line. Be sure to smile wider and more often than you might normally.

In most check-out lines (like those in grocery stores) you are strictly limited to the person in front of you and the person behind you. If all the lines are long and you have a choice, why not choose the line that has the most interesting-looking people in it, rather than the one that is going to get you out five minutes faster?

Here are some possible lines for when you are checking out:

"Oh, I love that stuff."

"It looks like you're having a party."

"Are you going to carry all that yourself?"

"Is this the express line?"

*"Have you been waiting long?"**

*"Do you ever wonder how much of our lives is spent in lines?"**

Ticket, restaurant, and movie lines: Waiting in line for an event is a good place to mingle, as you are waiting in line for something pleasurable. People are usually in an excited, anticipatory mood. Or, everyone is feeling impatient. A word of caution here: Most people don't like to hear other people complain about having to wait in line ("How much longer is it going to be, why don't they let us in") unless the comment is witty, or funny. Always remember, unless you are dealing with the Truly Arrogant, conversation while mingling should be good-natured.

Sample lines:

> *"Have you heard good things about [name of the movie or restaurant]?"*
>
> *"Have you guys been here before?"*
>
> *"I always feel funny, standing in these lines by myself!"*
>
> *"This better be worth it!"*

Ladies' room lines: This is by far the easiest line in which to mingle. Women standing in the seemingly endless, inevitable line for the ladies' room bond together with only the slightest encouragement, because all of them are equally furious at having to stand in line to go to the bathroom and probably miss the beginning of the second act as they always do. I've met some great people in ladies' room lines, but I find the conversation doesn't vary much. In fact, what I do in ladies' room lines is sometimes more like organizing a revolt than mingling.

Lines:

> *"When I become President, I'm going to totally revamp women's rooms throughout the nation."*
>
> *"I feel like just going in the men's room instead."*
>
> *"This is my idea of Purgatory."*
>
> *"If all the men had to stand in line to go to the bathroom for just one month it would change the world forever."*

Bank and post office lines: It's difficult to do any real mingling in either of these places unless something happens that draws people together (for example, if a machine breaks down). People are there to do serious, anxiety-producing business, and especially on an ATM line, people are wary of strangers. But I've still had some luck. Everyone is bored, even if they are also focused on whatever it is they are there to do. Note: It is okay to complain here. It often fits people's moods in these situations.

Lines:

> *"Money doesn't go very far these days, does it?"*
>
> *"You'd think with all this technology, this wouldn't take so long."*
>
> *"That's a nice coat/hat."*★
>
> *"I can't believe this; all I want is one stamp!"*
>
> *"Isn't it funny how we don't even think of actually going inside the bank anymore?"*

If you realize you made a mistake by talking to a particular person in the line, don't panic. You can still "escape," even though you naturally don't want to leave your place in line, especially if you've been standing there for a while. You simply have to turn your back on them. This sounds rude but it actually is acceptable for on-line mingling. Just pretend you are returning to a conversation with your friend, or that you are looking for someone across the street. If the person keeps talking to you, make believe you don't hear. This will probably shake him off. People in lines mingle very tenuously.

• Elevator Mingling •

I have always found it disturbing that people seem to have trouble talking to each other in elevators. We enter this little room, stand close together, stare tensely at the display panel, and breathe a sigh of relief when we get out. Most people tell me there's a good reason for this behavior: Our personal space is so infringed upon that our barriers are up. That's reasonable; after all, it *is* a very small space to be standing in. But if you think about it, you are standing no closer to people than you are at a crowded party. The difference is that you are in a tiny room that moves and does not seem altogether safe. Everyone is mildly anxious. Well—why not mingle away that anxiety?

It's the nineties, folks! We have to get over our elevator stiffness and take advantage of these golden opportunities to interact. I believe people are secretly desperate to learn how to elevate their elevator time. So if you're ready for new frontiers, here are the rules:

1. **Say hello.** It's important to greet everyone in the elevator as you enter, and also to greet people who get on after you. You'll be surprised at how people will warm up to this. Always accompany your salutation with a smile (your smile will have to be a bit more impersonal than one you would use at a party, especially if you are the only other person in the car. You don't want to scare anybody).

2. **Include the entire elevator in your conversation.** If you are getting into the elevator with someone else, or you discover someone you know in the elevator, don't ignore the others present. This will be a challenge for most, as people have always found it acceptable to have a conversation with another person almost as if there weren't four other people standing right next to them! I have always thought this behavior bizarre and alienating, and it's time it stopped. Your attitude should be that you and your friend have just joined a new group of people at a party. Turn toward the people already in the elevator (only slightly. Most people who haven't caught on yet to the proper social behavior in elevators will all be facing front, so your turn must be gentle). Make brief eye contact with people—as you greet them and then once in a while during conversation—but only for a

microsecond. The smaller and more crowded the elevator, the less eye contact you should make.

3. **Never make jokes about the elevator breaking down.** It's helpful to use humor to dispel the tension that exists in any elevator situation, and it is tempting to joke about cable breaks and electronic failures, but *don't do it.* It may get a laugh out of most people, but it could push the claustrophobic right over the edge.

4. **Talk about:** The sluggishness of the elevator, the decor inside, or the doorman of the building, if there is one. Also, if you are in an apartment building, you can comment on someone's mail (not personal mail, but magazines you happen to spot). For example, I once took a long elevator ride with someone who was carrying a copy of a computer magazine; we had a very nice chat about the best kind of word processor for a writer to buy. Elevator rides are, for the most part, short, so don't forget to begin your mingling when you are waiting for the elevator (heaven knows, that could increase your mingling time to fifteen minutes). Here are some lines to help you get started:

"Excuse me, but do you work (live) in this building?"

"Is there a thirteenth floor in this building? No? Isn't it amazing how that superstition seems to prevail?"

"We've all got to stop meeting like this."

"Do you lose your stomach in an elevator or is it just me?"

• Multigenerational Parties •

One trend in the world of parties is for people to bring their children with them. If you are over thirty and you're having a party, people *will* bring their children unless you tell them not to. This is a relatively new practice and one that is on the rise, so you need to know a few things about mingling at multigenerational parties.

Children usually add to, rather than detract from, a party. The obvious reason for this is the unending supply of subject matter they elicit. You can make observations forever. And talk about using flattery! You'll never struggle for a new comment about a strange pair of earrings again. The immediate avenue into someone's good graces is to praise his or her children. You may think the person will see right through this ruse, but they never do. Always remember that every parent, without exception, truly believes that his or her child is the most wonderful miracle that ever existed. And in a way, they're right. Children *are* wonderful, and they are fun to have at a party (as long as you are not the one who has to chase them around making sure they don't knock over the champagne glasses).

At multigenerational parties you are going to have to watch your language—and I'm not just talking about swearing, or crudeness. Each generation has its own lingo, and you are going to have to make certain that your audience is following you. Also, your mingling style will be much different, due to the fact that the usual standing clusters won't do. Many people will be sitting—some even on the floor (trying escape maneuvers from the floor will teach you the real meaning of the word challenge). You must offer to get the older people and tots refreshments, and offer your seat to the elderly. But make sure the recipient of your gesture really *is* old before you offer your chair; middle-aged guests may be insulted.

It's a sign of great progress, I think, that we are, as a society, leaning more and more toward parties, that include children, parents, and grandparents. Each particular age group has a perspective on life that is unique, and the greater the variety, the richer the mingling experience.

MINGLING IN THE NEW AGE

In many different social spheres throughout the world, people seem to be talking about spirituality and "New Age" topics such as astrology, channeling, healing, body work, yoga, shamanic journeying, and the Tarot. Since many people are interested in these topics, they may be an excellent source of subject matter for an enlightening and stimulating conversation.

If you are someone who generally balks at the mere mention of anything New Age-y, don't forget that often the most interesting conversations you can have involve philosophy or issues of the human condition. After all, would you rather hear about what someone bought at the grocery store yesterday, or what someone dreamed about? "Do you believe in psychic vision?" is definitely a more provocative line than "Do you come here often?" And in the wonderful world of mingling, you are not required to take anyone seriously; all verbal exchanges are for your amusement. So when the person you meet starts to talk about rebirthing, go with the flow.

On the other hand, if you *are* a proponent of today's New Spirituality, you may think "mingling" an outmoded institution belonging to alcohol-drinkers and other unwholesome types. On the contrary. Mingling is for everyone, whether the trappings include martinis or carrot juice. And if you are bringing the nineties "New Consciousness" to the art of mingling, you could be adding a much-needed spice to the old recipes.

However, you should be careful with whom you venture into these somewhat controversial subject areas. It can be a bit like discussing religion (that old taboo) and, more important, many people will think you are nuts. Try a test question to get a sense of your environment. A good one might be to ask the members of the group if they have ever been to a psychic. Psychics are a familiar concept; almost everyone has heard of someone who has been to one. You will be able to judge the advisability of entering into these "new" areas by the quality of the answers given. (It's not so much *what* they answer as *how*.)

Are their responses:

a) excited   d) sarcastic, or

b) inquisitive   e) abusive

c) nervous

If the answer is a, b, or even c, you know you can continue, but if it's d or e, retreat. Go back to talking about basketball, unless you are ready to be ridiculed.

But whether or not you are in the right crowd or the right frame of mind to allow your New Age interests to direct your choice of subject matter, there are other benefits to being a New Age mingler. Just think: You can use your psychic ability to help you perform like a seasoned mingler. Depending on your abilities, not only can you avoid even *approaching* undesirable types—drunks, the Truly Arrogant, and other obnoxious people—but you'll also sense just what to say for optimum conversational enjoyment, each time you face a new person. Of course, you'll be able to tell right away when you have come across someone with whom you have had a past-life relationship—a relationship that could be affecting your current conversation. (This experience is known as the Tingle Mingle.) And you'll be able to recognize, or at least suspect, when bad karma is slowing you down. But best of all, you can inject positive energy into everyone you meet, which is, after all, the aspiration of every mingler.

Mingling: THE NEW HOPE

I hope you have found the advice, techniques, and tricks in this book to be helpful to you in your mingling. Certainly, not all of the techniques will suit your personal style or circumstances, but if you are able to make just one of these min-gling devices a permanent part of your social life, you'll be well on your way to mastering the art of mingling. I encourage you to practice the maneuvers and gambits that appeal to you; you may find your aptitude for these techniques surprising. If you are a serious student of mingling, you may succeed in perfecting all the techniques in this book and becoming a freestyle mingler—inventing your own hand-crafted methods and lines. But however and wherever you mingle, always remember your number-one goal: enjoying yourself.

There may come a time when people will no longer need a guide to the art of mingling, a time when minglephobia has been completely eradicated. The need for survival fantasies will be a thing of the past, the Truly Arrogant will have been transformed into the Truly Angelic, and no one will ever think of the word "escape." Lying—even for mingling's sake—will be unheard of; perhaps we will even mingle telepathically!

By the year 2025, it is estimated that the Earth will hold 10 *billion* people—about twice as many as it holds today. That's an incredibly scary thought, given our dwindling resources. But as long as people are still interested in congregating in large groups for the pure satisfaction of talking together, there's hope for the future.

So mingle on!

INDEX

151

Counterfeit Search exit maneuver
and, 68–70

F

Fade-In entrance, 16, 117
Fade-out exit maneuver, 61–62
Fake It Till You Make It attitude, 1–2
Fanaticism, talking politics and, 138–139
Fancy things, reacting to, 88
Fans, using as props, 96
Fantasies, surviving mingling using, 3–7,
124
Faux pas, dealing with, 107–116
Fear of mingling
    mingling with people with, 122
    overcoming, 1–11
    panic, handling, 129–130
Flattery, 16–19
    arrogant people and, 124
    mingling with minglephobics using,
    122
    reacting to, 89
Food
    Buffet Bye-Bye exit maneuver,
    67–68, 126
    conversations about, 34, 36, 102
    Hors d'Oeuvre Maneuver, 100–101
    spilling on someone, 73
    working the food area, 101–103
Free association, changing the subject
    with, 76–77
French accent, using a, 88
Fumbling In gimmick, 84–85

G

Games, playing as a mingling technique,
    39–40, 86, 119
Gimmicks for mingling, 82–90
Giving up and leaving, 130–131
Glaze-out, 28, 57
Glowing, conversations using the
    expression, 34
Good Samaritan exit maneuver, 67

Gossip, 44–45
Graceless artfulness, 84–85
Groups, safety in numbers with, 10–11

H

Hand-kissing, lines to handle, 127–128
Hand shaking, 12–13
    Honest Approach entrance and,
    15–16
    Shake and Break exit, 64–65
Hats, using as props, 95–96
Helpless Hannah Ploy, 41–43, 121
Honesty
    Honest Approach entrance, 14–16,
    117
    recovering from a faux pas with, 26,
    111–113
    Honest Approach exit, 61
Hors d'Oeuvre Maneuver, 100–101
Host/hostess
    conversations about, 34
    getting introductions from, 80–81
    mingling as, 103–105
Human Sacrifice exit maneuver, 65–66,
    121, 126
Humiliation, dealing with, 25–27, 58
Humor
    conversations about, 35
    elevator mingling and, 146
    faux pas, dealing with, 110
    guidelines for using, 52–53
    jokers, handling, 53–54
    recovering from a muffed opening
    with, 27
    saving face, 58

I

Ice, conversations using the expression,
    34
Illness, pretending, 73
Information, requesting, 41–42
Insults
    fielding with a toast, 90

155